C0-DAM-015

'Your Best is Good Enough'

'The Art of Forgiveness'

Guilt-free, Self-help Guide to
Holistic Healing, Spiritual Growth and Miracle-
healing of
Mind, Body and Character
without Stress with the
Bach Flower Remedies,
Clear Thinking
and
Words of Power.

Lorenzo Peays-Mills

Copyright: © Lorenzo Mills 1998

Cover: Evelien Philippa

Printed in the U.S.A.

ISBN 0-9663908-7-3
Power Flower Publishing

No part of this book may be reproduced in any form, by print, photoprint, microfilm or any other means without written permission from the author.

*" Everyone of us is a healer, because every one of us
at heart has a love for something."*

Dr. Edward Bach, '*Heal Thyself*'

Dedicated with my deepest love and gratitude to Master Maharaj Charan Singh Ji and His heir Gurinder Singh Ji of Beas, India without whose Grace this small work would not have been possible.

Also, my special thanks to Evelien Philippa for her unending patience and work. She helped with typing, editing and advising at every stage of this work as well as designing the cover.

Only Cheryl and Scott know how much they mean to me. Further, thanks to Jamie and Friso and to all my special friends in Holland.

Also, thanks to all those at the Edward Bach Center in England and especially to John Ramsell for his advice and help throughout the years. I hope we'll meet face to face one day soon.

Special thanks to Dr. Edward Bach for the great work he did and his example of love and humanity. He was truly blessed by God and I am grateful to contribute in my small way and spread his light. 'Standing on the shoulders of giants.'

Lorenzo Peays-Mills
's-Hertogenbosch, the Netherlands

Contents

Foreword

This book is an attempt to shed light on the dark side of the moon. An attempt to spread the art of forgiveness, for ourselves and others. Practical examples and not theory is my "Modus Operandi". Hundreds of healed people give me courage to speak out against everything I learned in school. Study the examples that are given in this book and make your own affirmations or 'video's' and see how simple things can be.
Draw your own conclusions.

Remember... true happiness lies in acceptance and contentment.
Your Best is Good Enough! What more can you do?

Lorenzo Peays-Mills

*"The greatest gift that you can give to others is
to be happy and hopeful yourself; then you draw them up
out of their despondency."*

*"The action of these remedies is to raise our vibrations and
open up our channels for the reception of the Spiritual Self; to
flood our natures with the particular virtue we need, and wash
out from us the fault that is causing the harm. They are able, like
beautiful music or any glorious uplifting thing which gives us
inspiration, to raise our very natures, and bring us nearer to our
souls and by that very act to bring us peace and relieve our
sufferings. They cure, not by attacking the disease, but by
flooding our bodies with the beautiful vibrations of our Higher
Nature, in the presence of which, disease melts away as snow in
the sunshine."*

*"There is no true healing unless there is a change in outlook,
peace of mind, and inner happiness."*

Edward Bach

The Tale of the Dastardly Duo

'A house is not a home'...

Inferiority feelings can control, diminish or even destroy someone's life.

If these feelings become a part of our personality they can grow and grow like an unstoppable infection until all self-confidence and even physical health has been damaged or destroyed.

Physical beauty, education or intelligence, talent or warmth of personality all lose their value in the face of this hungry monster.

It never ceases to surprise me how many of the rich and famous suffer from this disease of self-esteem.

Feelings of _INFERIORITY_ and its twin, **_GUILT_** have become masters at worming their way into their victims' home just like termites. These tiny, innocent seeming insects left unrecognized and unchecked can quickly multiply and spread to every nook and cranny of our home.

The weak or sick parts as well as the strong and healthy parts of our home or personality is attacked.

They weaken or devour everything in their path until the very foundation of our health and happiness is threatened.

They have an inborn desire or rather instinct to survive at all costs like every living creature in Nature.

Camouflage, fear and denial are their chief allies.

They are immune to almost all drugs, therapies, discussion groups, logic or common sense.

Mistakes, doubts, criticism from others (positive or not) and self-criticism comprise their main diet.

Physical or mental _'inadequacies'_ real or imagined increase their fertility ten fold.

They are extremely poisonous and should be considered armed and dangerous.

Even the admired and expensive homes could be infected without the conscious knowledge of the resident.

Tell tale signs of their presence are often found in the vocabulary. Expressions like *"I'm sorry", "I should have known I couldn't do..", "That's too good or too high for people like us", "I'm so ugly or stupid, etc."* or constant apologies or defense for accusations that have never been said or implied by others usually betray the presence of these treacherous twins;

INFERIORITY and **GUILT**.

To truly control and eliminate these parasites we must completely eradicate them.

We must go down to the very foundation of the problem and we must also be able to identify and destroy their breeding ground to protect the health and happiness of our home in the future.

With the help of the flowers... of course.

"A house divided against itself cannot stand."

Jesus Christ

"If we learn to control the desires of the mind we make spiritual progress."

Maharaj Gurinder Singh Ji

Philosophy

People often say to me that they don't understand my philosophy and my way of life. They come to the conclusion that I never have any problems or that I just sit on my butt the whole day. Some even think that I'm cold, hard and indifferent.

They miss the point. They're looking so hard, they can't see. Dr. Bach who knew how the human mind works wrote the following beautiful words:

"Let not the simplicity of this method deter you from its use, for you will find the further your researches advance, the greater you will realize the simplicity of all Creation."

"Take no notice of the disease; think only of the outlook on life of the one in distress."

"Final and complete healing will come from within, from the Soul itself, which by His beneficence radiates harmony throughout the personality when allowed to do so."

Edward Bach

Dr. Bach's Flower Remedies are based on the philosophy that most of all sickness have a mental or psychological cause. In other words, most sicknesses are psycho-somatic... caused by the mind worked out through the body!

Most of what we assume to be true about the nature and origin of sickness is WRONG. Bacteria, germs and cold weather should be relegated to a supporting role. Worry, fear, hate, jealousy, shock, loneliness, shyness, bitterness etc. etc. play the leading part in causing sickness.

The Bach Flowers are comprised of 38 different flowers, trees and plants such as, pine, oak, honeysuckle, chestnut, clematis, holly etc. Every flower has a certain influence on our character and emotions. Every person receives a different combination of flowers according to their mental and emotional problem. By strengthening the positive characteristics the negative side of the character is healed. Light and darkness can not exist in the same place. Logically it follows if sickness is caused by negative characteristics then their elimination would automatically increase positive characteristics which would bring about a cure.

This theory has been proven through my experience of seventeen years of wondrous healings. Just a few drops of the essence of plants or flowers mixed with spring-water can improve and often heal many physical, mental and emotional problems which we normally consider to be incurable.

It's strange how many people are not afraid to use habit-forming drugs or expose themselves to cancer-causing rays or painful operations but are scared to drink a few drops of 'rose-water'.

These flowers are simple and safe. Overdose is impossible and even if you take the wrong flowers the only thing that happens is they don't have any effect. It's perfect. When light enters a room, darkness disappears.

These are called wonder-healings but if you understand the higher spiritual laws which govern this process then it's just as natural as TV or radio. For people who've never heard of TV it must seem like a miracle too. Actually, most of us don't understand how TV or radio work. We use it everyday until it becomes normal and normal things are not noticed. In the beginning days of television people were afraid to have this new invention in their homes because they were sure that the program-makers were looking in their homes. Many women were afraid to get undressed in their own homes. They were sure they could be seen and heard at *"television-headquarters"*. If you'd been born deep in the jungle and had never had contact with the modern world, you'd never believe in tubes with wings that carry people through the air or little boxes where whole orchestras and bands played when you pushed a button. There are other boxes where people talk and move and even die only to reappear the next week! Anyone with such a box would be called a magician or a fool. I'm called both.

Your best is good enough is a philosophy that is so simple, it's sometimes difficult to see. Millions of people who think they are incurable could be helped by a fast, efficient, safe and cheap method without side-effects or danger.

Almost every person or disease can be effectively treated with the Bach Flower Remedies and so few seem to be willing to try to understand. In my own surroundings it is difficult to even give the Flowers away. Many people I've healed refuse to speak to me later out of fear or ignorance. They think if they admit to being healed by the Flowers then the cause had to be psycho-somatic which of course many mistakenly equate with faking or being crazy and nobody wants that. They refuse to admit to being healed or they stop with the treatment after enormous improvements. The better and faster the improvement, the more afraid many people are. It's a strange world but it's not their fault. It's not anyone's fault but it's important to be aware that your mind might try unconsciously to sabotage your healing out of fear or some kind of resistance.

Must everything be difficult and complicated to have value for us? It seems so but people who are difficult and demanding are usually avoided. Easy-going people are usually loved and happier. Happy people are healthy just like the song: *"Don't worry, be happy."*

Every *'do-it-yourself'*-improvement book, every psychologist, every neighbor and friend gives us the same advice. Most people already know what they need to do... the problem is how to do it. Making checklists and saying to yourself a thousand times a day

"I'll be rich, I'll be rich" is not enough. Not everyone can be rich or win the Olympics.

If a loved one has died or doesn't love you anymore or if your arm has been cut off, it won't return because you say *"I want it back, I want it back"*. Please understand I'm not trying to make anyone ridiculous. All these methods have their advantages and many people have been helped. BUT: those individuals who are able to carry out these self-help programs or who are willing and able to work 18 hours a day will become rich anyway and don't need these programs. They will probably be rich or die trying. Any fool who thinks that being rich or famous is more important than health or happiness should be cured and not encouraged.

Healings will continue until the general public realizes what a blessing God has bestowed on us in the form of the flowers. The Bach Flower Remedies will be the healing method of the future. In this book I want to share the wonders of my fortunate work. Hopefully you'll benefit by the experience.
We're all just doing our best.

Please forgive me for any mistakes I might make, they are entirely of my own making and reflect my personal short-comings and not any weakness or incompleteness of the Bach Flower Remedies or those who now lead this worthy organization.

"A glorious view opens before us! We see that true healing can be obtained, not by wrong repelling wrong, but by right replacing wrong, by good replacing evil, by light replacing darkness, we come also to the understanding that we no longer fight disease, that we no longer oppose illness with the produce of illness, that we no longer attempt to drive out maladies with such a substance that can cause them. On the contrary, we now bring down the opposing virtue which will eliminate the fault."

Edward Bach

"Our deepest fear is not that we are inadequate, our deepest fear is that we are powerful beyond measure. It is our light, not our darkness that frighten us. We ask ourselves, who am I to be brilliant, gorgeous, talented and fabulous? Actually, who are you not to be? You are a child of God. Your playing small doesn't serve the world. There is nothing enlightened about shrinking, so that other people won't feel insecure around you.

We are all meant to shine, as children do. We were born to make manifest the glory of God that is within us - it's in everyone. And as we let our own light shine, we unconsciously give other people permission to do the same. As we are liberated from our own fear, our presence automatically liberates others."

Nelson Mandela, Installation Speech 1994

The true cause of sickness and disease

Dr. Edward Bach M.B., B.S., M.R.C.S., L.R., C.P. D.P.H. (Camb.) was a famous and honored physician and homeopath who was born in Wales and worked and studied in London, England. In medical circles he's still well known by his development of a treatment of intestinal problems that is still used over all over the world.

In other circles, he's known for a system of healing known as the Bach Flower Remedies. These are the essences of 38 various flowers and plants which are aimed at curing negative mental and emotional states.

In spite of his fame as a doctor and researcher and a thriving practice, Dr. Bach became increasingly aware that certain sicknesses seem to be connected to certain emotional or character types. At a certain point he could successfully judge which patient was suffering from a certain disease by just observing this person or speaking to them for a short time, without discussing their medical history. This confirmed his growing feeling that sickness was connected to the mentality and character of the patient. It became more and more difficult for him to prescribe harmful drugs to his patients or to recommend surgery which he knew would not give a lasting cure.

As he devoted more and more time to spiritual research and meditation, his clairvoyant powers increased tremendously. He gained a spiritual insight into the Oneness of Man, Nature and God. He began to see sickness not as a curse but as a warning or learning tool from our 'higher'- or spiritual self to our 'lower' or material self or personality.

What good is there in attacking the physical body with drugs or knives when the true culprit hides in safety in the dark recesses of the mind and emotions. Modern science and medicine has become the God of modern man in the last centuries.

Unfortunately, this God has feet of clay. Instead of improving our lives and eradicating sickness it has turned on us like a hungry shark. *"The operation was a success but the patient has died"* has become all too common and acceptable.

The drugs that were welcomed as our saviors have them-selves become the source of sickness and suffering. Just read the side-effects of 'simple' medicines for headache, stomachache or even simple aspirin. It's enough to make you sick or scare you to death before you take them. These medicines don't cure the problem or the sickness but they do create new problems and sicknesses both physical and emotional. Heart-problems and thromboses are often a result of hormone-treatments or long usage of the pill.

Dr. Bach saw this coming and said to one of his colleagues: *"Now, I have to forget everything that I have learned"*.

He became convinced that there had to be a natural, simple and harmless cure for sickness. He devoted more and more time to meditating and wandering the woods in search of flowers and plants which would do just that. At a certain point he could hold the pedal of a flower or the twig of a plant or tree in his hand and feel its healing powers.

Many flowers that are used in homeopathy and in other flower- or herbal healing methods are poisonous or harmful if not used properly. These, Dr. Bach immediately dismissed.

His ideal was a safe, cheap and effective system which could be used by everyone without any medical training.

While in a self-induced trance he took on every imaginable sickness and symptom and wandered in the woods in pain searching for the right plant that would cure it. Many times he laid near death. Persecuted by the medical profession which once called him 'genius' he refused to give up his ideal. Driven by his love for God and his desire to help relieve the suffering of humanity he gave up his health, fame and material well-being to develop this system, known as the Bach Flower Remedies.

Personally, I could never have been so strong. As he discovered his flowers, he put them to immediate use and quickly cured many people, often miraculously.

The books by Dr. Bach are so pure and simple that I can not imagine anyone reading them untouched.

Books by his companion, Nora Weeks, and others that worked directly with him and later followed in their footsteps, are highly recommended.

There's no mysticism or magic involved in a correct treatment with the Bach Flowers. Personal insight, is of course necessary as in everything. Tarot-cards, pendling, using muscle-tests, letting the patient choose the flowers from photographs or passing their hands over the bottles are, in my opinion, unnecessary and misleading. A simple talk or description of the sick person should be enough, just as Dr. Bach and his followers have been doing with success since the Dr. Bach's death in the 1930's.

Clouding the issue with ceremonies or rituals only detract from the miraculous powers found in the Flowers when used in the proper way. If the Flowers are used in the right way there should be many miracle-cures of a wide range of problems and sicknesses. Thereby, many more will be cured in a less spectacular but steady way.

Hahnoman, the founder of the homeopathy once said:
"there are no sicknesses, only sick people."
This puzzled me for a long time and it wasn't until I read Dr. Bach that I realized what he truly meant. It's the character and the mentality of the person that attracts and creates sickness. '*Disease*', taken apart is *dis - ease* or uncomfortable.

A disagreement or conflict between our higher- or spiritual self ; which desires only good and love and our lower- or material self which desires only gratification of the Ego or self, material comfort and wealth at the cost of anyone or anything. It's not personal. It's a kind of built in self-gratification drive which is stronger than we are.

This conflict or rebellion against the Divine Will filters down to the mind and from the mind to the body, creating what we call disease. There is a difference between our outer 'face' which we show to the world and often believe ourselves and our true or inner 'face' which for social, moral, financial or whatever reasons is hidden.

The greater the difference between these two the more tension is created. This 'dis-ease' or tension is like a spy hiding in a Trojan horse who opens up the door to sickness. Stress, fear, hate, anger, bashfulness, trauma, jealousy, shock, worry and guilt are the keys which opens the door of misery.

In many old movies it was not uncommon for the heroine to faint or go into labor at the news that her love was injured or missing in action. That people died of heartbreak was not considered to be so strange.

People who refused to be cured because they had given up their will to live would be miraculously cured when their lost dog returned or their loved-one who'd been missing in action was found. Dying of a broken heart was something that everyone could understand. To understand is not to cure; that is now possible with proper use of the Flowers. Nobody has to *"pine away"* because of a broken heart.

For the list of 38 Bach Flower Remedies, see page 186.

Good and Bad Medicine

Nowadays, viruses and bacteria are pointed out as the bad guys. Doctors look at us with a straight face and tell us that the patient died of *'heart-failure'* or *'respiratory arrest'* (which will kill you every time).

It's the old scenario of the operation was a success but the patient died. Clearly, the interest of some doctors and the interest of the patient and their family have often become separated along the way. An operation where the patient dies can never be a success. The sickness and the patient have been forcibly disconnected and are seen as two separate entities but they are not. There is no such thing as a small operation.

The danger of side-effects, narcoses and shock are ever present. Do you *cure* a gall-bladder problem by cutting out the gall-bladder? Or solve a menstruation-problem by a hysterectomy?

A leading surgeon said that 99% of the hysterectomies performed in America were not done because of cancer- or life-threatening situations! They were performed to 'cure' menstruation problems and pain. Instead of searching for a true cure or simply admitting that they don't have an answer to this problem many millions of women, their husbands and families have been made to suffer and pay and pay and pay.

Unfortunately, we have to realize that medicine and business have become one. Careers and financial kingdoms are built and depend on the continued sickness of a frightened public. When it is a case of the patients' gall-bladder or uterus or doctors' second home in the country or luxury car, unfortunately, the choice is all too often a material one.

Fortunately, not all doctors or medical personnel fall into this category. There are many that are truly dedicated to healing but they are becoming fewer and fewer in number. Joining the medical profession because of tradition, financial reasons or other material concerns has done untold harm.

Materialism has turned the medical world into a God-like hierarchy where self-serving tradition has become more important than the patient. 'The cathedral is completed but the people are dead'- kind of mentality. Because of the high costs of training and medical equipment, doctors have been- in many cases- forced to sell out their ideals. This situation will change.

The big business of the pharmaceutical industry and drug sellers have taken over. In a certain country, the problem of curbing unnecessarily expensive medicine met with such a resistance from the powerful medical associations that nothing could be done to cure this problem.

It was only when insurance companies complained over high costs were allowed to refuse to pay for expensive medicines where there was a cheaper and just as effective alternative available that change began. It turned out that many of these medicines were exactly the same except for label and price. Only then, did doctors begin to prescribe the cheaper variation.

In the same line, questions were raised that many pharmacies were being supported by international pharmaceutical companies which paid doctors and pharmacists 'bonuses', etc. for prescribing various expensive and often unnecessary medicines. The Minister of Health in question replied that this was a known and regrettable situation but that they couldn't just stop it overnight or 50% of the pharmacies would go bankrupt. This is a situation that exists in many other countries.

I have nothing against pain-killers or drugs. They are sometimes necessary. Why suffer? We must realize that these are dangerous substances and that surgery is a radical and traumatic experience for the patient and the loved-ones and it should not be resorted to lightly. I believe dangerous or experimental medication or surgery should be the *last* step to be taken, not the *first*.

Informed patients Heal Faster

A social psychologist followed a hundred patients who were to be operated. He found those patients who received direct and clear answers to their questions were less nervous or afraid before the operation and on the average, this group was released one day earlier than the group of the uninformed group of patients. Dr. Breemhaar concluded that weeks after their release from the hospital, the informed group of patients were more active than the other group. Mental attitude and motivation were cited as the reason for this. The psychologist tried to motivate hospital personnel to give more information and be more open to the emotional and psychological wishes and needs of patients. He received little or no cooperation. *"The motivation of the specialists was much less than optimal"*.

We must take a certain responsibility to see what is happening around us and to us. We must Think Clearly and use everything in our power to help ourselves before strong medicines or operations are necessary. When this is inevitable, let us try to soften this as much as possible by Clear Thinking and the correct Bach Flowers while **working together with our doctors**. The Bach Flowers are not meant as a substitution for Medical Care.

In a foreign newspaper I read an article called:
"Higher Cancer Risk in Hospital"
Hospital personnel such as doctors, nurses and pharmacists, assistants who were involved in the preparation and administering of cytostatica have a higher risk of cancer. Cytostatica is used in chemotherapy treatment. They are "biologically active" and can cause cancer. In spite of preventive measures personnel are still in danger.

The Bach Flowers can be successfully used with any and every other medicine, therapy, treatment or diet without any side-effects or dangers. What greater gift could be given to us?

Dis-ease... we don't feel comfortable with certain circumstances or certain people. We're simply not comfortable with ourselves. This dis-comfort expresses itself as disease or sickness in a physical, mental or emotional way. It's actually a spiritual problem. Those who search outside are in error.

Patients must wake up and help themselves. Being a 'patient' is fine but if the root of the problem is not taken away how can there be a definite cure? If we refuse or are afraid to look inside or don't know what we're looking for then we're still lost. We must have the means and the ways necessary to do the job. We must do it and not talk about doing it.

'Patients' cannot do this, they are *'patient'*, they wait. Patients do what they're told and things happen TO them. They don't understand usually what is happening to them or why. They take little or no active role in their own cure so they heal much slower than is possible in many cases. They take no active role so naturally they cannot actively and consciously work to cure or protect themselves from sickness and discomfort in the future.

If there is something a 'patient' can do to help heal themselves why shouldn't it be used? Especially if there are no negative side-effects as in the case of the Bach Flowers.

Every step is a step. You can treat the flower, the branch or the leaves of a plant but if the root isn't healthy the plant will not be cured. The old problem will come back or a new problem will be formed. This never stops unless the root is cured. If the root of the problem is cured all problems will disappear.

We cannot defeat physical death. I'm going to die as we all are. There's no guarantee that I won't ever get sick or be depressive but I do know what I can do to get myself out and if that's not possible to be given the strength to accept my destiny much better. That's worth quite a lot too.

'What can't be cured must be endured.'

"Those who kill will in turn be killed, whether they kill for food or for sport. Meat is the food of dogs, not his who is blessed with the human form.
Advising people to eat grains and vegetables, Kabir says:

Who eats grain is a man,

Who eats meat, a dog;

Who renders the living being dead

is a devil incarnate.

Kabir, *the Weaver of Gods' Name*

Words of Power

Affirmations have been helpful to some people. Positive thinking is a hundred times better than negative thinking.

Everyone would probably agree with that but I think **OBJECTIVE THINKING** is a thousand times better than positive thinking! Positive and negative are only opposites of one and the same entity or thing.

Heads and tails are different sides of the same coin. If we have heads, tails can't be far away. That is a law of nature. Fat-thin, ugly-beautiful, old-young, black-white, up-down, man-woman, life-death, etc. are all tied to each other by the law of opposites. As long as we have one, the other must appear sooner or later. Positive thinking is the opposite to negative thinking and therefor always tied together. We can't escape it.

This world is the world of change, of opposites of Yin and Yang. The only true escape or peace is to be objective or neutral in our thinking. The ground of the world is covered with the thorns of hate, jealousy, fear, anger, greed and uncertainty.

As Maharaji Jaimal Singh Ji said: *"These thorns can never be completely annihilated."*

But if we put on thick boots we won't have much trouble enduring what cannot be avoided.

Just as nature has her cycles and seasons so does life. No mantra, visualization exercise or affirmation can change that. The birth and blossoming of spring and summer, the aging and death of autumn and winter. All have their function and place in God's plan. Some people live in places where it is almost always summer and some where it is almost always winter and the most somewhere in between. Still, everyone experiences happiness and unhappiness, loss and gain. There is no escape. Only those who have become detached from the seasons are truly permanently happy. Those who walk the spiritual path under the guidance of a truly Enlightened One pierce the veil of duality which we call *'life'*. They accept what cannot be changed without losing their balance in this world. They realize this is not our True Home and don't try to possess what is and can never be theirs. These lucky few imitate the ducks who swim in freezing water without getting wet or feeling cold.

They make use of the water, are in the water but they don't fool themselves into thinking they can *'own'* or *'conquer'* the water. Ducks have been given a thin coat of oil over their bodies which insulates and protects them against the elements. The oil separates them from their environment. They swim and float in the water but don't get wet except superficially. If this layer of *'objectivity'* is destroyed by pollution or whatever the water seeps in and they become so water-logged they can no longer float or fly and they sink and drown. If they do make it to shore their insulation against the cold is gone and they freeze.

In the same way we are so overloaded with cares and fears we can no longer protect ourselves from the inevitable disappointments of life on earth. We lose our protective layer and are denied our true destiny.

Bound to the earth by our many attachments we begin to forget the ecstasy of free-flight. Caught in the contradictions of material law and daily existence we are thrown from attachment to attachment. Our wings are broken. We go from mountain to valley; light to dark; life to death and back again. No man or woman can change or hold back the seasons but we are helped by realizing and admitting their existence and dressing accordingly. Become like the duck. We can rise out of the murky water and fly away.

"Everything we see in nature that we call destruction is really creation, going from creation to creation."

John Muir

"You think the shadow is the substance; so, to you the substance has become a cheap toy. Wait until the day that substance freely unfolds its wings. Then you will see the mountains become as soft wool and this earth of heat and ice become nothing; you will see neither the sky nor the stars, not any existence but God - the One, the Living, the Loving."

Rumi

The mind has become blinded by emotions and wishes of one kind or another. This has gone so far that we can no longer trust what we think or know or think we know. The Words of Power are based on common sense and common experience.

It's been cushioned with intellectual words and theories and it sounds quite true but no one can always get what they want when they want it. It's exactly what our material minds and empty material lives need. *"I am God", "I am the master of my destiny"*. It sounds good but in reality this proves to be an illusion. Even when we get what we want we usually don't want it anymore or it turns out to be very different from what we thought. So why think so much? Be logical. Be safe.

Repeating something a million times a day doesn't make it happen or stop it from happening.

Wake up! Grow up!

Naturally, we must put in the effort and do our best but let's not be too fanatical. Let's not sacrifice our health and happiness just to *'have something'* or *'be someone'*. We already have something and we are already someone.

Aesops' fables are a great source of inspiration for me.

This is a story I love to tell workaholics and sport-fanatics.

It's about a baby frog who ventured outside his pond into the pastures for the first time. This was strictly forbidden but he was so curious he couldn't stop himself.

He came to a fence and there he saw the biggest, strongest creature he'd ever heard of. He thought his father, the bull-frog, was the biggest creature in the world. This new animal was called a bull. The little frog stared at it in amazement. Forgetting his possible punishment he hurried home to tell his proud father what he had seen. *"Father, I saw a monster!"*.

When the father heard this wondrous story he was angry. Even though he himself had never been beyond the pond he was convinced that no such creature could exist. To prove his point, the bull-frog puffed himself up bigger than his son had ever seen before. *"Was he bigger than this?"* asked his father triumphantly.
"Oh yes, much bigger than that, Father" the baby-frog answered. All the other frogs stared in amazement.
This only made the bull-frog angrier and he took several enormous breaths. *"Bigger than this"* his father asked with his eyes bulging out of his face. *"Even bigger than that, Father!"* the baby-frog said. The father, determined not to be outdone this time, took another deep breath and puffed and puffed and POW! He explodes into a thousand little pieces.

"Pride comes before the fall." Yet, each stone, each creature or living being is distinct, individual and irreplaceable. The world doesn't revolve around any of these creatures except perhaps, in their own egotistical minds. Our own egotistical minds.

Whole civilizations, cultures and kingdoms have been created and disappeared without a trace and a tree is still a tree. Where are the great Greek, Roman, Egyptian, Persian, Maya, Inca cultures? Name as many as you like, they are now nothing but dust. Are our petty wishes and desires more important than whole cultures? We know the answer but we don't act like we know it. A slave is not free and has no choice but to try to please their master or suffer the consequences. A slave owns nothing except what is given by the master. One glance from the master and home, partner, children and *"possessions"* can be destroyed or taken away. One telephone call can take us to the mountain-top of happiness or send us to the very depths of despair depending on the news. That is reality. We can't change life so let's try to accept it without illusions of grandeur. We do our best in all humility and hope for the best. For without humility we can never have inner peace or happiness.

" In truth everything and everyone is a shadow of the Beloved, and our seeking is His seeking and our words are His words. . . We search for Him here and there, while looking right at Him. Sitting by His side, we ask: "Oh, Beloved, where is the Beloved?" Enough with such questions. Let silence take you to the core of life. All your talk is worthless when compared with one whisper of the Beloved."

Rumi

Devoting 10-20 minutes a day to peaceful contemplation would do wonders for our health and outlook on life. Repetition of the three sentences which follow will bring a certain amount of objectivity to life around us. After all, the tensions and problems in life are created by our own visions of them.

"When you got nothing, you got nothing to loose." It doesn't matter if we really have anything to loose or not it is the attitude that matters. The more you have to loose, the more fear and tension you have and therefor you will perform less efficiently. The old saying; *"it's not whether you win or loose but how you play the game"* is very true and goes much deeper than many of us realize. Let us concentrate on how to play the game and forget winning or losing.

1. *The Past is Past*
2. *Destiny is Destiny*
3. *Your Best is Good Enough*

I like Star Trek and tonight's' episode of Star Trek's Voyager had a scene illustrating how our emotions work. Captain Janeway and Chakotay were infected with an unknown and dangerous virus and the crew was forced to leave them on the planets' surface to avoid contamination. Tuvok, like his pre-decessor Spock is a purely logical Vulcan who were able to gain control over their emotions generations ago.

Tuvok is second in command and has to take command of the ship. Everyone aboard feels guilty and sad about leaving their conrades behind even when that's the only *logical* thing to do.

Tuvak: *" I fail to see what you expect of me"*
Officer: *"Clearly something you can't do."*

Tuvak: *" And that is?"*

Officer: *" To feel as rotten about this as the rest of us."*

Tuvak: *"You're right. I can't feel that particular emotion and frankly, I can't see what good it would do."*

While the rest of the crew was suffering, the logical Tuvak, was not. He was protected from emotional turmoil and pain. Naturally they succeeded in finding a cure before the end of the episode after the necessary trials. Clear the mind and heal the body.

"The emotions are the enemy"

Bruce Lee

1. The Past Is Past

For many people the past has a powerful attraction and influence. This power is almost magical. A sound, a smell, an event or a thought is enough to trigger a whole array of different memories and/or emotions. We've all had that experience of a wonderful or horrible memory being triggered by a song, a perfume or an odor...

All these feelings, sights, sounds and ideas are lying dormant in us like a time-bomb or a "sleeper" spy waiting to be activated by the secret code-word. Whether this agent will hurt or help us is not in our hands. We are not consulted - they just come.

Their favorite weapons are:

1. The *'WHY'-question*
2. The *"I shouldn't"* or *"I couldn't"*-torture
3. The *"I should have"* or *"I could have"*-torture
4. The *"those were the days"* -illusion

Still others are not trapped in the past because of traumatic or horrible events but are happy volunteers who cannot forget how fine and simple things were "then". Possibilities of happiness or action now no longer exist for them. Whether crippled by accident, sickness or other causes, the only important point is how to heal our injured bodies, minds or souls and resume our lives. After all, a broken heart, a broken trust or spirit can be just as painful as a physical injury and usually twice as difficult to cure. Sometimes we have to give up memories that may be precious to us when they create or support our sickness. That's not easy. Trapped animals will sometimes chew off their own paw to free themselves from a deadly trap.

So many problems of today and tomorrow have their roots in the past. Consciously or subconsciously many people live and relive their past, their youth and according to many even their birth and beyond.

Nothing is so sad or frustrating than to make or see someone else make the same mistake again and again...

This mistake could be getting angry or being afraid of some person or situation or it could be trying to punish some person or yourself or... etc. etc.

There are millions and millions of variations according to an individual's life and experience. What makes it all the same is we usually can't do much about it. Therapists and medical people often tell us we have to learn to live with it but we can't. Sometimes we're told exactly the opposite by positive thinkers who tell us we could change if we only really wanted to enough or learned a certain lesson.

One of the main problems is that we're not always allowed to change or improve from ourselves. Old images, experiences and complexes are difficult to shake. Especially when our sub-conscious is either hiding them from us or disguising them as something harmless or even as something positive. In reality it can be negative images of ourselves or our world which cause us to suffer, become sick or fail in relationships or work.

Often I've had clients who've been mistreated, abused as children or wives, victims of crimes and accidents and who are totally convinced that these misfortunes are somehow they're own fault. These people, for the most part (99%), were victims and somehow their mind has convinced them that it was their fault and that they must therefor pay for their crime or stupidity. They are not allowed to change because they are imprisoned by the past.

The origins of some sicknesses are anchored in these kind of ideas so the answer to curing these various sicknesses and problems lies more in changing these ideas than anywhere else. How many times have we seen people in negative relationships or problems with the law or whatever because they feel they don't deserve any better and therefore can never have any better. Forget about logic. When there are unconscious forces at work logic is usually made useless by the same power that keeps this problem alive - the unconscious mind.

"Don't touch shit! Not even with a ten foot pole!"

The past usually means bringing up old pain, regret, fear or whatever so let's leave it alone, unless there's a very definite, concrete reason. Don't touch it because when we repeat an experience in our minds, the pain, fear or whatever from that experience very often comes with it and even becomes stronger.

However, in the real world that just isn't true. No two circumstances will ever be exactly the same. Neither are we always the same, even in similar circumstances. Emotions, mentality, weather, what we heard or saw just before the situation or after, all play important and often unknown roles in determining or forcing a certain action or reaction. Digging up the past won't help us unless we also have a method to cope with it and cure it.

An American humorist once said: *"It ain't the things we don't know that cause all the trouble in life. It's the thing we think we know but ain't so."*

If we haven't learned our lesson in a few months of thinking and pondering over some action or situation why continue for years and years? Especially when we see the pain and grief we do to ourselves or others. On top of that, we create fear to feel or act in the future because of *"mistakes"* in the past. It's the domino-theory once again.

Not only do we feel the pain or whatever from the first mistake but we continue to suffer for it in the present and in the future. Fear paralyses us. *"Once bitten, twice shy"*. We are constantly pursued by the memories of the original problems. It's like digging off the scab of a small scratch every time it almost heals

41

for years on end. The original wound doesn't heal and you run a real danger of infection now.

Often, we become so obsessed with the past that forgiveness in any form is impossible. There is a great personal price for this.

No one wants to make mistakes or be wrong but no one is perfect except the True Masters. Let's expect to make mistakes and be wrong from time to time. Try to avoid mistakes but when they do occur try to recover as fast as possible and move on. Life becomes so much easier and enjoyable for everyone. That heals. Give wounds time to heal in peace but don't forget the past is past.

There can be no spiritual development or personal progress without love and there can be no love without forgiveness and charity. Living and re-living wrongs done only keep the negative feelings from that time alive and strong. This is a great mistake and only serves as food for hate, anger, fear, revenge and the other enemies of health and happiness.

All parents make mistakes. All children make mistakes too. Some of these mistakes are devastating and cause traumas that can follow us and destroy our lives, our future. Continuing to think about these things or fearing them day after day and year after year is like chaining yourself to a sinking boat and entering a swimming contest and expecting to win. There can only be one result. Too many people are still suffering because they survived the war while loved ones or others did not.

Fifty years later they are still paying for something which lives only in their own unforgiving minds.

It's not always conscious but the damage to them and their families is the same as if it were.

I've treated Jews and Germans successfully for this problem with the Bach Flowers. Survivors of car- or other accidents and all variations on this theme should be taking the Bach Flowers in combination with support groups or other chosen therapies.

Once you've talked about a problem ten times it should be clear that talking just don't cut it. Do something. Let's stop cursing the darkness and light at least one candle. If you feel like these people mentioned above or you've been raised by people who carry this load, please try the flowers. If your partner suffers from this help them repair the emotional damage you've probably all suffered and move toward the light.

Asking people to forget about the past doesn't help. Pleading with them to forget about the past doesn't help. Screaming at people to forget about the past doesn't help either. To forget about the past Bach Flowers help.

Forgive others and more important, **FORGIVE YOURSELF. THE PAST IS PAST**, **close the door and move on. . .**

Get rid of the past anyway you can !

Why? . . . because Destiny is Destiny, that's Why !

"Past is past" usually gets head-shaking approval because that's often visible and therefor considered logical. *"Destiny is destiny"*, on the other hand, is always a pretty bitter pill to swallow for 'Western' minds. *"Because"* is not considered to be an intelligent and acceptable answer to a *"WHY"* -question in our culture. Teachers become angry when they hear it. Adults consider me childish and unrealistic when they first hear it. Later, they realize it's a kind of intellectual quicksand. The harder they fight, the quicker they sink.

In their mind's eye they see me begging for mercy after being cut to pieces by a few sharp, humiliating and humoristic lashes from their razor-sharp tongues. My philosophy, if any intelligent person could call it that, had about as much chance as a snowball in hell, according to them. The on-lookers join in when possible with supportively smile and urge them on to the intellectual kill while exchanging open looks of approval.

Recently, I experienced this situation exactly as described above. While doing a television interview in Amsterdam, I met an American psychologist. A Ph.D., leading man in his field, noted scholar, author, etc. He had it all, it seemed. He was here on tour, holding seminars in his special area. He had severe neck-pain due to 'worn-out disks'. He insisted nothing could be done because his specialist had said... I cut him off at that point and gave him a few drops of the appropriate flowers. I also gave him one of my massages and he felt better immediately. He couldn't believe it.

His brother was killed in a traffic-accident a few years before and the pain of that was still bothering him, according to me. Also, he was still bothered by some painful experiences when he was seven or eight years old.

Life is in our own hands and we can shape and form our own future, he insisted. After all, that was the topic of his lectures.

If we can shape life and control our own destiny as the famous psychologist professed why does he still have trouble about things that happened when he was seven years old?

After 60 years, it's still there, in spite of diplomas in psychology, affirmations, etc. The doctor had no logical answer to these questions but he still steadfastly held on to his idea or rather illusion of personal power. He wanted to debate the point but I felt his inability to change his own life proved my point. The atmosphere was heavily charged. Debating only hardens feelings and nobody's mind is ever changed by it so why bother. I took my leave and headed for the train station. Two minutes later I heard my name being shouted.

My friend, the psychologist had been robbed. His bag was gone along with his passport, credit cards, a large sum of money and very important names and addresses. We made a token search but found nothing. I went with him to the police to help with the language problem and for moral support.

He canceled his credit cards, called his insurance company and did the necessary things.

I was sorry for him but at the same time thankful to be witness to such a beautiful and clear example. It was like God had put on this demonstration just for our benefit.

Most people have read and followed the advice of all these self-help books, mostly written by psychologists which tell us to get rid of old baggage and take life as a lesson. These books advise us to see the good in everything, etc. What happens if you can't force yourself to think positive? Then you're in deep trouble because these books have no answer for this. Most of us start off with enthusiasm and end up disillusioned and depressed. The various techniques and programs are limited in vision and scope. They function outside of reality and real life. Things don't always work out as planned. Count on change.

Sometimes these changes are insignificant and they are sometimes matters of life and death. Large or small, it happens all the time to everyone. We call it *'good'* or *'bad'* luck, chaos, angels or coincidence. I call it destiny.

Very often great *"discoveries"* are made *'by accident'*. While looking for one thing often a totally unexpected other thing is discovered. These discoveries are often made by other amateurs, hobbyists or students. Why?......because!

A perfect example was on CNN the other day (June '97). A famous mathematician had been studying and working to prove something called the Fermat Theorem. Day and night, he worked on this problem for seven years. Finally, he thought he'd found the solution. A formula which would concretely prove this Theorem. Mathematicians all over the world have been trying for the last hundred years but no one has been able to do it until now.

The mathematical world was ablaze with excitement. Kind of like winning four gold medals at the math Olympics.

The whole scientific world was watching and even beyond that closed brotherhood the attention was tremendous. Publicity was inter-national. The problems came after this formula was presented to other mathematicians who were asked to check it point by point. There was a mistake found.

Now, the man who had loved working on and studying this formula for years could now hardly look at it. The next six months, he said, were harder and more stressful than the previous seven years. His dream had become a nightmare. He decided to give it one more day before giving it up and admitting defeat. He was looking at his initial approach and studying the work of a Japanese scholar when he had this *"revelation"*. Everything became clear and very simple. He found his mistake! Why didn't he see this three years ago when he first studied it so diligently? Who knows. He had that article with the *"answer"* right there in front of him the entire time without seeing it. Just when he was about to give up he saw it. *"In a flash"* he saw the solution, he said, it was a *"revelation"*. There were tears in his eyes. It was not an intellectual discovery but a spiritual one. He was:

> *"Looking so hard you can't see"*

Lilly Belle Hannaham-Peays

Destiny is a very strange thing.

Did you know that the American telegraph pioneer and inventor Elisha Gray, worked years on a method of transporting the human voice electronically. In other words, he worked on the discovery of the first telephone but he wasn't meant to be *'the one'*.

On 14 February 1876, he filed for a patent on his new invention. Unfortunately someone had beaten him to it.

Alexander Graham Bell had filed his patent **two hours earlier.**

Not only that but Bell wasn't trying to invent a telephone. He didn't want to change the world. He was searching for a tool to help deaf children understand the nature of speech and sound. The missing link. Bell needed to make his invention work was provided when he *"accidentally"* spilled some battery-acid and gave Bell the answer. God had already decided who's going to do what, when and how.

His decision is called DESTINY.

He uses people and situations to implement his Will. Standing in the quiet of the woods, looking at the stars, in the middle of a big storm or any act of nature; being close to mountains; these are the things which give us a true sense of proportion of ourselves. It makes us realize how smail and unimportant we really are. Learning humility saves much pain and grief for those who are allowed to see it.

"Whenever a new discovery is reported to the scientific world, they say first: "it's probably not true"

Thereafter, when the truth of the new proposition has been demonstrated beyond question, they say: " Yes, it's true, but it is not important."

Finally, when sufficient time has elapsed to fully evidence its importance, they say: "Yes, surely it is important, but it is no longer new."

William James

"Our ego and pride stand in our way and make the mind powerful and strong. It is humility which will rid us of our ego and self-importance. All saints teach us this lesson in their writings. What is our value after all? What is the individual's value in this vast creation that the Lord has created? Billions of universes like ours lie within man, the microcosm in this macrocosm. Our existence, that of the individual, has absolutely no value and we should not attach much importance to ourselves."

Maharji Charan Singh Ji

Destiny is destiny - Things happen...

Most of us are brought up with the idea that we can do anything if we want to. If we don't get what we want we didn't want it enough or we didn't work hard enough. It sounds logical. It sounds plausible but in the real world it's just a bunch of useless words.

Every athlete who tries out for the Olympics and participate for their country know only one person, normally speaking, can win. Many of these men and women have scarified everything for the possibility of victory.

They've trained and endured pain and injuries for years, sometimes even had surgery for the chance to participate. Many have sacrificed other careers, money, relationships and health and still most of them will win neither fame nor fortune.

Can we be as heartless and thoughtless to say they didn't want it enough? It's ridiculous but many people do. It's said about children who fail in school or sports or adults who fail in business or relationships.

We accuse others of it and we often accuse ourselves as well. What we are really doing is creating millions of unhappy people. Unhappy with second place, unhappy with third place. Unhappy with their own personal best and unhappy and dissatisfied with others as well. Guilt and inferiority-complexes destroy happiness and health by taking away the most valuable thing we have in this world... namely a positive self-image and feelings of self-worth.

For those who are sick, peace, hope and harmony are the greatest gifts we can give. Of course, we are seldom in a situation that lends itself to those virtues. We don't live in this heaven-like tranquillity surrounded by peace and love.

Just as in the animal- and plant kingdom, the struggle of survival is the rule. This being the case, it's on us to try to create an oasis of peace within ourselves in spite of and in the midst of this struggle. Taking a few minutes each day to picture ourselves in some peaceful quiet place does much to achieve this. Imagining ourselves to be above and beyond depression, pain, fear or the irritation of others helps us to feel just that.

Those few, who have the blessing of true meditation under the guidance and protection of a True Master know the truth of these words. Still, seeking inner peace in our own way in the quiet of our own home goes a long way and is very important to our health. Warm foot-baths are also very soothing and help to evaporate tension and troublesome thoughts which destroy inner-rest. I recommend all these things in combination with the Bach Flowers. Inner peace and health are one.

Supreme Being, Creator, God or whatever name you give It or Him has put us here for a reason. Not a material, earthly reason, but a spiritual one. We, like everything in existence is endowed with Holy Spirit, a Soul. As such, we are all sacred and worthy. Not every stone can be the corner-stone but how could you have a solid building with only corner-stones? Impossible.

So every stone has its place and purpose. Whether it knows it or not, it's just as important as the corner-stone or the shining marble. Not everyone has the destiny of greatness or fame or the gift of intellect, health or beauty but still, we all have our place and individual importance.

Acceptance of this is very important to health and happiness. It's essential! Even in the vastness of creation every creature, plant or grain of sand is like its' kind and at the same time explicitly unique and individual. Sand is sand, yet when examined closely, we know that no two grains of sand are exactly alike. Sand by the ocean is different from desert-sand or sand in the mountains. The Inuit of Alaska make a distinction between 30-40 different kinds of snow. Each has its own name and characteristic.

Tension, a fear to win or an unconscious guilt-complex etc. can keep people who've trained years for a certain event or moment from winning.

The race in sports as well as in life is actually won or lost before the race is run. Our attitudes about ourselves and the pressure and attitudes from others around us often unconsciously decides our fate. It is not a question of wanting to win or not. Neither is it a question of guilt or innocence or physical ability. Destiny has decided the result long before the race takes place.

I remember a certain woman athlete who, in my opinion, suffers from a serious self-esteem problem. My heart sank before the race because I'd followed her career for years and had often thought if she'd been under treatment with me she'd have been World Record holder and Olympic Champion long ago.

I was convinced she suffered from inferiority complexes and fear. Even though her best time -in less important races - was far better than the competition she could never win the big events. She'd never allowed herself to win. She'd either get disqualified for false starts or she'd fall. Once she was sure she was going to win she'd pull a muscle or get an injury or she'd tense-up and slow down until the second place runner had passed her and then she'd begin to run again only to loose by a few inches.

I'd seen it happen before. After being 10 yards ahead she'd visibly slow down to -what looked like- a almost still-stand until the second place runner caught up (finally) and won.

What a shame. I think she could use the flowers desperately. She could still accomplish much in the athletic world. Much more importantly, a change in attitude would make her a better and happier person and a better athlete.

These kind of invisible problems are responsible for a great deal of emotional and mental pain. They can often be quickly cured with the Bach Flowers. Years of psycho-analysis and digging in the past, self-crucifixion or crucifixion of the parents offer no real cure. If that was true, Woody would have stopped playing 'pocket-pool' years ago!

How many people suffer incredible pain and uncertainty in their hearts because of a lack of sympathy or understanding. So often in daily life our wishes and goals are thwarted. We're too late for an important appointment, we said the wrong thing, we 'let' ourselves get angry or ...or... or... What can we do? It's like working on an assembly-line. We don't have the power to decide how fast the line moves or what products come down that line but we do have to work there.

So we do the best we can with what we have. We can only hope the people in the line ahead and behind us do their jobs but it's not in our hands to decide for them.
It doesn't matter how much we'd like to help them or how important it is to us to be perfect or how much we worry nothing is changed. Let's accept our destiny and have peace with the fact that we've done our jobs as well as we could and not be worried about the result. If we think we should make a suggestion or do something then do it and do it quickly.

However, once the arrow has left the bow there is nothing to do but wait and see if we've hit the mark. We've done our best and now we must go to the next step and not worry or feel guilty or whatever. All of our decisions in life, positive and negative have already been decided. Our youth, our talents, our weaknesses, our astrological sign and the stars we're born under, our environment and our so called heredity have already been mapped out so run the best race you can and forget about winning and losing.

Destiny is character and character is destiny. God is an invisible power who works His Will through and with people and circumstances. There is no such thing as chaos. Chaos is only a spiritual or hidden law that is as yet undiscovered for material thinkers. Only our mind and ego blinds us from the truth.

The thought, the action and the result of the action are all predestined and are an expression of Gods' Will in the material world.

"Once, a Guru tried to make this principal clear to his best student who happened to be the king. The Guru pointed out that destiny or the Will of God decides our fate and not our 'own' will or desire. The king, however, stubbornly held to his belief that if he tried hard enough he could do anything.

The Guru insisted that nothing can be if it is not the Will of God. Nothing that happens, positive or negative, can happen unless it's the Will of God. The king still felt he could decide and guide things. The Guru got up quietly and left.

After a few days he returned to the court of the king. He walked in unannounced, sat down on the kings' throne and ordered the king to be arrested and thrown in the dungeon.

The guards stood perplex and didn't move. They knew how much love and respect the king had for his Guru. The king knew the Guru sometimes did strange things to force him to think or look at things in a different light but this was going pretty far.

The Guru, however, seemed serious and repeated his demands. Now, the king, being insulted, could take it no more and angrily ordered the guards to arrest his Guru and throw hum in the dungeon which they did.

Confused and troubled, the king couldn't' sleep. The words of the Guru kept circling through his head until he finally couldn't *take it anymore and went to the dungeon in the middle of the night. The Guru explained it to him.*

Anyone can sit on the throne and imagine they're the king. They can give orders and make decisions but the ministers and guards will only obey the commands of the real king. It doesn't matter how much the impostor wants something or how correct it seems to be, unless you're the king or his appointed agent, nothing will happen. In a flash, the veil of ignorance (Ego) was lifted and the king understood (was Enlightened)."

We try to guide and control others, life and circumstances without any success. We can't even control our own thoughts and still we live in this illusion of free will, choice and power. We sing songs we hate and ten seconds after stopping we start singing the same song again. We buy products we don't want or need and speak of being able to do anything in life if we want it bad enough. Where is this power to decide destiny and life?

Honest objective thinking proves none of us have it. Impostors on the throne. Why not admit our weakness and at least enjoy the many benefits given to a friend of the king.

Destiny is Destiny

Psychologically speaking, it sometimes seems that people who are pushed by difficult circumstances can perform beyond their normal limits. We must and can go farther, faster, higher, longer etc., etc.. Champions are made in this way, we are told. Ninety-nine percent perspiration and one percent inspiration is said to be the formula for genius and success. Albert Einstein didn't agree. He said that his mathematical and scientific discoveries were a result of spiritual inspiration and not mental or intellectual endeavor. The man considered to be the smartest man of our time says clearly that his intellectual accomplishments had little to do with intellect and I believe him. The record of discovery and invention in all fields in all times prove that fate had chosen certain people to do certain things at certain times and nobody and nothing can change that. Check the history behind the discoveries and you'll be amazed how often an invention or the solution to a problem blocking an invention is discovered or solved by coincidence or accident, the answers are sometimes found in a dream or 'revelation'. "Eureka!"

"When you don't know whether to laugh or cry;
it's better to laugh. Life is too short."

Lorenzo Mills

"The short passage on this earth, which we know as life, is but a moment in the course of our evolution, as one day at school is to a life, and although we can for the present only see and comprehend that one day, our intuition tells us that birth was infinitely far from our beginning and death infinitely far from our ending. Our Souls, which are really we, are immortal, and the bodies of which we are conscious are temporary, merely as horses we ride to go on a journey, or instruments we use to do a piece of work."

Dr. Edward Bach, Heal Thyself

Your Best Is Good Enough
- Karma -

In my practice, I'm often confronted by people suffering from many different sicknesses, complexes or problems which often all come from one problem or variations of the same problem. This Hydra, this five-headed monster is called 'Guilt' with a capital 'G'. This beast has many faces and they are all ugly and deadly.

The mind is nothing more than a computer and like a computer is can only print out what has been programmed into it. There is no computer on earth that can begin to compete with this living machine we call the "mind". Nor is there any machine to compare with this perfect vehicle used to transport what we call the "body". Computers are built for different purposes and functions. No matter how many beautiful functions and talents a particular machine (person) may have there are also always imperfections built in to it. Mental, physical or emotional.
On the other hand, no matter how flawed or imperfect a particular computer (mind) may be there is also always something beautiful and perfect about it.
As a believer in re-incarnation, I believe that individual computers are consciously or unconsciously drawn together or thrown together according to set programs determined long before they physically came into contact with each other.

As an astrologer who has predicted many, many detailed and accurate events in the lives of strangers by studying the stars, I can't believe in a free will. At most, I can believe in a very limited free will that was exhausted many thousands of lives ago. Now our souls are programmed or indebted to perform certain actions; experience certain re-actions and have particular feelings for people that are pre-programmed by actions from former lives. All decisions have already been made.

This system of programming and pre-programming is called "karma. In this way, God makes sure every computer only gets what it truly deserves; "An eye for an eye and a tooth for a tooth." We could also say "you reap what you sow."

Karma is just a way of spiritually balancing the books. Every cent is accounted for even if we don't remember making it or spending it. Spiritually speaking, no one ever wrongs us or treats us unfairly. We all deserve everything we get according to past thoughts and actions. Isn't that a comforting and logical thought? That's more logical than thinking life is chaotic and unfair because God is asleep at the controls.

"Some people go trough tragedy without being much affected by it, other people pass through the same tragedy and start howling and crying. For both of them the tragedy they have to face is the same, but not its effect; that is dependent on their spiritual and mental development. Certain people are so spiritually developed that they are not bothered by what is happening, though they may be facing a tragedy day and night... and meditation help us in that we become spiritually strong within ourselves and do not lose our balance in undergoing such karma's, we do not feel their effect."

Maharaj Charan Singh Ji - 'Spiritual Heritage'

The concept of guilt is difficult to defend when looked at it in this way. Please understand, I'm making a distinction between higher spiritual guilt and earthly or judicial guilt. A person found guilty of breaking the law will be punished. If, when, how and who will be punished is determined by fate, not by individuals. This would certainly explain the many injustices found in our human judicial system. We shouldn't make it personal. You stick your finger in a fire, your finger gets burned. It's not personal. Fire burns everyone.

Our health is damaged by the effects of negative emotions. If we break the law we are punished. The spiritual laws, unlike judicial law, plays no favorites. Race, religion, finances and connections play no role. Nobody escapes the eye of karma. We forget what we have done in past lives as the soul moves from one body to the next but the karmic bonds are inescapable.

"Judge not, less ye be judged" is a statement of the karmic law of God. *"Do unto others as you would have them do unto you"* is more than a pretty platitude. It is a statement of spiritual law and truth. Remember the Lords Prayer: ...*"forgive us our trespasses as we forgive those who trespass against us"*.

In light of this who is free to cast the first stone? Only the Holy Men and Women are but they do not because they realize we know not what we do.

Forgiveness and love is their rule. All are paid back in the same coin. Soldiers who kill of necessity induce no guilt or obligations of karma as long as the emotions play no part. As soon as hate or pleasure etc. come into the game it becomes personal and we are held personally responsible.

Those who wish to make spiritual progress are urged to become vegetarians by true adepts. Killing for the pleasure of killing or the pleasure of taste buds make a debt which must be paid. How can we say there is no justice in life? If we don't want to pay we must try not to harm any living creature unless out of self preservation or necessity otherwise we will have to pay for it.

Everything that happens has a past history so what is good and what is bad? Who is guilty and who is innocent?

Who is the victim and who is the true perpetrator?

There is no way to justify hate.

Remembering death can strike at any given age or time will help us put things in their true perspective. Insults and injuries of major proportions shrink to their true insignificant size when we think of karma and death. A human being is so small and weak. We should forgive ourselves and others was well. The computer in our head which we call the mind is very cut and dry: 'guilty people are punished'. Sickness is often a case of self-punishment for real of imagined crimes. Forgive yourself and others.

We have always made mistakes and in spite of the best intentions, we always will. So let us become better Christians, better Moslems and better Buddhists or Sikhs. Human beings who forgive are the true believers.

"Equations, words, thoughts, concepts, beliefs, theories, intuitions, expectations, dreams. All of these are smoke, too wispy to support you. This book also is smoke, but it points in the direction of Spirit's fire. Burn up your fears and uncertainties in that divine flame. Drown your ignorance and misconceptions in that holy water. This is why you were born - to die and be born again. This time as the eternal essence of Ultimate Reality."

'Gods Whisper, Creations' Thunder'

Happiness = Health = Happiness

We only have to read the 'boulevard-press' magazine to see which movie-star is on a crash-diet, had a facelift, is divorced for the twelfth time or has tried to commit suicide to realize that success is no replacement for happiness or health.

If Elvis was not happy or healthy in spite of all his success then it seems clear to me that happiness and not success should be our goal.

I have nothing against success. I hope to sell two million books but if my book is never published or if the only copy sold is to my mother I am still going to sleep well.

I could get depressed, hate myself or society and become a terrorist and bomb publishing offices or develop mysterious pains in my writing arm, get an ulcer or bronchitis or I could say; "my best is good enough" and try again. The glass is half full or half empty, it depends on how you look at it.

A customer of mine had been suffering from extreme pains in the knees for 22 years. After 3 operations she was advised to have an artificial knee inserted. According to me, her problem with the knees came from a guilt-complex. From childhood she had been forced to work very hard and like many people with similar problems the only time she was allowed to rest was when she was sick.

The programming from youth continued to work unconsciously so that every time she took a rest, the pain would come back even worse. "Only lazy people sit on their butts", "Empty hands are the tools of the devil", etc. I've treated this women for several years with varying success. There always seemed to be an invisible wall between us. It was as if she didn't want to be healed. It was as if she was protecting the cause of her sickness. After so many wonder-healings, I couldn't understand why certain people would stop with treatment just when it seemed they were about to be healed. I began to suspect some unconscious resistance.

When she came to my office she had such pain in her knees, she could hardly walk the stairs. She laughed and said she had already found a solution which she often used at home. She sat on the stairs like a small child, and pushed herself backwards step for step up the stairs. It was a sad sight. I was determined to find the true source of the problem. We came to talk about her parents once again.

It seemed that she had a love-hate feeling for them which made her feel very guilty. The discovery of an extra-marital affair her husband had, 22 years earlier, was the beginning of the problem with her knees. Feeling that she had failed him and the children she began to 'punish' herself in the form of excruciating pain in her knees. She wanted to run away but her feeling of guilt and duty wouldn't allow it. With the use of my *'Words of Power'*:

1. *Past is past ... move on*
2. *Destiny is destiny... things happen*
3. *Your best is good enough ... you can't do anymore*

I tried to make it clear to her that she had done everything humanly possible, therefore she couldn't possibly be guilty.

Since the past couldn't be changed anyway it was senseless to continue punishing herself. All of a sudden she jumped up and said she had to go home and make warm chocolate-milk for her children who had been having trouble sleeping.

When I reminded her that her children where over 30 years old and quite capable of fixing their own milk she replied that she was still their mother no matter how old they were. The woman ran down the stairs, taking them two steps at the time. Later, I heard her 30-year old daughter was angry with me because her mother wasn't home in time to warm her milk!

For two weeks she had no pain in her knees at all. When it came back she didn't want to continue the treatment. When I spoke to her she said that her 'good knee' gave her much more trouble than her 'bad knee'. I explained to her that maybe her 'bad knee' wasn't so bad anymore and this was a very hopeful sign.

The next time I heard from her she had her artificial knee and the pain was worse than ever.

The glass is half empty or the glass is half full, depending on how you look at it. People who say it's half empty have regrets about the half that is gone and don't see the half that still remains. People who say that the glass is half full have already enjoyed that half and are looking forward to the other half. They're both right... half is half. But one way of thinking is negative and gives us tension which eventually will make us sick. The other way is positive, makes us content and strong and will eventually heal us.

Many people have been programmed to see guilt in every thought and action. They see guilt as a positive way of the mind to help us 'learn'. Many people do not permit themselves to fail. They consider it failure to accept help from anyone except maybe a doctor or an operation.

Very few people will ever allow themselves to be healed. Therefor we must recognize this fact and deal with it in a positive way.

The Bach Flower Remedies, the *'Mills Video Technique'* and the *'Words of Power'* is a complete way of healing and (re-) programming ourselves in a conscious and positive way. We must fight not to allow death, failure, shock or trauma from the past to dominate and control our health and happiness today.

Most doctors admit that 70-80 % of all their patients are sick because of mental or emotional problems and yet almost nothing is done to discover and cure these psycho-somatic causes.

I developed the 'video'-techniques to replace the old unconscious programming of the mind with a conscious and positive 'film'. By repeating this 'video' 2 or 3 times a day for 5-10 minutes at a time will produce amazing results. They're personal and they're fun. We're constantly fooling ourselves without realizing it. With the 'video', we can put this characteristic to use in a practical and positive way.

Affirmations

Affirmations or positive thinking have their limits. Contrary to what many best-selling psychologists say, we do not have the power to control our destiny. Making lists of our wishes and sticking them on the doors and refrigerators sounds good but in reality it is nothing more than wishful thinking. If the wished-for goals aren't reached it creates false hopes leading to frustration, anger and sometimes depression or collapse of self-confidence.

"I'm going to get rich, I'm going to get rich", stuck on the mirror will not put money in your hands. It's not always the best musicians who get to be number one. Many "successful" people have reached positions without ever wanting it, or working towards it. People with the fastest times, don't always win every race either. Even when your wish is granted and you become rich that is no guarantee to happiness. There are essentially two questions to be asked:
1. *What are we really asking or wishing for? and*
2. *Will it make any difference in our lives?*
Wishing or 'ordering' something or someone by thinking about it 3 times a day will not make it happen. We can't make ourselves one inch shorter or taller. We can't extend our lives or the lives of loved ones one second longer than ordained. Think about it. If we could get our wishes just by wishing harder the grave-yards and hospitals would be empty.
No one would be lonely, sick, ugly, old, afraid, childless (or maybe they would be) or whatever. Only a spoiled child thinks that they can have what they want whenever they want it. The problem with spoiled children is they're never satisfied. The mind is also like a spoiled brat. It only wants what it doesn't have and as soon as it gratifies one wish it immediately throws that wish away and wishes another and another. Besides that, the

mind usually attacks the one who has spoiled it as well as anyone else who gets in its way because they're used to thinking the whole world turns around them. Such a child can never be happy or satisfied.

Happiness doesn't mean the fulfilling of wishes or richness, beauty or anything else. Happiness lies in contentment. Do the best you can and be content with the result. Riches brings the curse of ego, fear and greed. Jesus said "it's easier for a camel to go through the eye of the needle than for a rich man to enter into the Kingdom of Heaven". Someone rich and successful usually doesn't want to hear that their success is a question of Karma or Gods' Will and not one of personal achievement or will-power. Pride and Ego won't allow it. Living for material or egotistical goals can never bring happiness. Even when we achieve these goals we will not be satisfied but be driven to the next desire and the next.

"Rich man looking for another million dollars, poor man looking for one."

Mothers' Finest, Satsang Music

Without inner peace and spiritual contact, everything is meaningless. Most of us know the story of King Midas:

King Midas was very rich and ruled over a mighty kingdom. When approached by a fairy and allowed one wish, he wished that everything he touched would turn to gold. He was the happiest man on earth... for a while. The king touched a cup of clay and it turned to pure gold. Midas couldn't have been happier. But when he tried to drink some wine, it too turned to gold. Midas was the richest man on earth but soon he was the thirstiest and hungriest because all the food he touched turned to gold. He called his beloved daughter to him to ask for help. Before he realized it he touched her and she also turned to gold. The king cried and prayed the magic fairy would return and allow him to take his wish back. He realized that in stead of being rich he had lost everything of value in his life; his daughter and his health. Of course, the fairy took the wish back for King Midas had learned the true value of love. Midas was content.

I have nothing against money and hope to have a little of my own one day but inner contentment helps us to keep our balance even in those moments of life when we must struggle and fail.

Can money heal a broken heart? Being lonely in one room is bad enough but being lonely in 30 rooms is worse. Although we wish for many different things at different times in our lives all we really want is inner peace and contentment. A starving man will cry out for bread, cake, meat, soup, fruit and a thousand different dishes but all he really means is food of some kind. It doesn't matter what kind of food it is.

The mind is just using many different names for the same thing. Being content is more important than being successful.

What good is it if we gain the world and loose our own soul?

The mind, or no. 2 is as I sometimes prefer to call it like a wild monkey in the trees...

He jumps from here to there and from one branch to another. He is uncontrollable unless you know the secret. The hunter knows the monkey and knows his weakness. It's by this knowledge that he's able to catch the monkey.

Wild monkeys are caught with desire. A jar filled with sweets is placed under a tree full of monkeys. A rope is tied around the jar and attached to the tree. The hunter waits patiently for his victim. When a monkey discovers the sweets he sticks his hand in the jar trying to grab as many sweets as he can....

Then, Catch 22, the hunter suddenly appears and the monkey tries to get away. But his hand is stuck in the jar and he can't get it out. The poor monkey looses his freedom, his family, his home and everything that makes his life worth living. He doesn't get the candy either.

You ask yourself why the monkey couldn't get his hand out of the jar, he had no trouble getting it in. Simple, his fist, full of candy was too big for the opening of the jar as planned by the hunter who knows his quarry. All the monkey had to do was to let go of the sweets and take his empty, relaxed hand out to escape. But greed and panic made him forget this simple fact and everything is lost.

"I want" ties us like the monkey is tied. "I feel" paralyses us like the monkey and so we are slaves to our senses and desires, to our families and our "possessions". We are tossed between happiness and sorrow for 60 or 70 years and then we die without ever having being satisfied. Only when we see that jar of sweets for the poison it is can we begin to protect ourselves and those around us. Only those without desire are happy and free in this world. The rest of us are prisoners or our minds and our minds are prisoners of our senses and desires. The mind is never satisfied so we go on and on.

Taming a wild monkey isn't easy but it can be achieved through patience, love and knowledge, if it's our destiny to do so.

Since most of us don't know our destiny we can only do what we can and hope for the best. The rest only makes us sick. The mind is our worst enemy but once tamed, it's our best friend.

Inability to fulfill wishes created frustrations and complexes. Contentment is the absence of desire. The less desire, the more contentment and freedom. Intelligence can't help us here. It only gets in the way. For example, thousands of people are wounded or killed in America every year with unloaded guns . . .

I hear you saying; *"How can people be wounded or killed with unloaded guns?"* Well, it goes like this, someone has a gun and points it at someone else. The one facing the gun is rightfully frightened and asks their friend not to point the gun at them because it could be loaded. The person with the gun insists that it isn't dangerous, they're sure the gun isn't loaded.... BOOM ! Someone's dead. *"But I thought..."* says the friend with a smoking gun in his hand.

Thinking is not enough. We have to KNOW. True knowledge is only gained through experience. Never point a gun at anyone thinking it's not loaded because what we think is not always what is. Thinking is good but knowing is better. Until we know through direct experience it's a good idea to leave open the possibility that we could be wrong.

Many people have the idea that complete happiness or inner peace would be boring. It would keep us from being creative. We'd be lazy if we lost our drive to achieve our goals. Unfortunately, the people who say such things have never experienced real peace.

When you're contented you can't be bored because you don't want or need anything. Words like *"positive stress"* makes as much sense to me as *"Jumbo-shrimp"*. I always wonder if people who believe in positive stress believe in *"positive heart-attacks"* or *"positive high blood pressure"* too.

Many big businesses are beginning to agree with me in this. They're devoting a lot of time and money for relaxation. Yoga-classes and seminars devoted to teaching personnel how to relax. Some even provide child-care services. Weekend-seminars, bio-feedback classes, camping weekends to solidify and strengthen relations in the workplace. Big businesses have realized what yogis and Masters of the East have known since time began.

A relaxed and contented atmosphere helps to make a relaxed and contented person. Such a person is more creative and productive. Such a person is seldom sick in contrast to a high-power, beefsteak-eating, alcohol-drinking, high blood-pressured, dissatisfied, heart-attack waiting to happen executive of the classic type. (whew!)

As far as I know there is no way to change character and mentality except for the Bach Flower Remedies. Once you have a certain character or habits through birth, environment, circumstance or experience, you're stuck with it according to medicine, science and the general public.

Psychiatrists even say "the words 'to heal' doesn't exist in psychiatry". They spend years of treatment at crazy prices without ever really curing the problem. I'm not a strong believer in psycho-analysis because very few people are ever truly cured and many people become addicted to harmful drugs (medicine). The worst part of all is that all kinds of garbage and negativity is dredged up from the past with no means of dealing with it besides pointing an accusing finger at ourselves, our parents or someone, etc. Thus causing more problems.

The original problem is still unsolved plus many old problems are added. The flowers, used properly, could put an end to this kind of thing and help so many who now live in hopelessness and despair.

The flowers can be used in combination with any and all therapies or treatments thereby increasing the positive points of every therapy without any damage.

Do we have a task in life ?

So often clients say they feel frustrated or disappointed because they feel they're not fulfilling their task or destiny. Either that or they're afraid they'll miss or won't discover their task in life. That's impossible because God has planned every event in life whether we know it or not!

Our own egos have convinced us that we must all do great things and change the world or our lives have had no purpose. As if we could have the same comfortable life if we didn't have someone to bake our bread or make our clothes or educate ourselves or our children.

Everyone of us has a purpose and goal in life. We are all needed in some way.

Great scholars, inventors, healers and spiritual leaders have come and gone and still the world is more or less the same and has continued without them. I'm sure the world can get along without us too. Whole peoples and civilizations haven come and gone without our ever having known they existed. Only the human ego makes us believe this illusion of self-importance.

If asked about reincarnation most people are convinced they were Cleopatra, Napoleon, Caesar or an 'Egyptian High-priest' or 'Priestess', etc.

Nobody was ever the stable man or the cleaning woman. We're like one of those one-day-flies who're born in the morning; go through puberty and mating in the afternoon and dies at sundown. Still, that fly feels it's had a full life and cared for the continuation of its kind. A million eggs are fertilized and half a million is eaten right away by some other bug who happens to be passing. This all happens a million times a day, the entire summer long, without us ever having realized or cared that they lived or died.

The sun rises and sets and life goes on. Except for our feelings of self-importance we are just about the same as those flies. For most of us our task in life is to live and work normally wanting more than we'll ever have or need.

Alexander the Great arrived with his victorious army in India during his world conquest attempt. Having heard there was an advanced soul staying near-by, Alexander went to the yogi to ask for spiritual advice. It is said that the art of palmistry was brought to the west by Alexander the Great after he burned the library in Egypt.

The yogi was sitting under a tree in deep meditation with all his worldly possessions next to him. One bowl for food, another for water and a walking-cane. He worn a thin loincloth as his only wardrobe. The Conqueror approached in his golden armor with his staff of officers and demanded some proof of the yogi's spiritual power and advice.

The yogi looked at the youth, smiled and sank back into a deep trance, oblivious to the world of material affairs and ego. Once again, Alexander, demanded attention and promised to make the yogi king of that entire region in exchange for some spiritual help. The holy man only smiled.

When promised his weight in rubies, there still came no answer. Now Alexander drew his sword and threatened to cut off the man's head if he didn't break his silence and obey.

Still smiling, the yogi answered that he had no interest in being king or being fabulously rich because a rich mans' life is no longer safe; not even from his own family and friends. As far as losing his head, the yogi said he knew when and how he would die and it wasn't that day nor was it by Alexander's sword, so he had no fear.

74

His life was devoted to the spiritual world and he had no interest in the Temporary toys of material people. The Great Alexander realized how foolish he'd been and asked the yogi if there was anything he could do to express his thanks for this subtle lesson and wise advice.

The Wise-one asked if Alexander could please step to the side because he was blocking the warmth of the sunlight. At that moment, a soldier hurriedly approached and told Alexander that his men were in rebellion.

They'd been gone from home for two years fighting for riches and Alexander's dream and now they wanted to go home and see their families. If the army didn't start for home the next morning, Alexander and all his officers would be murdered that night. The army broke camp the next morning. On the way home Alexander became sick and realizing he was dying, he offered the half of his empire to anyone who could guarantee him he could see his mother one more time. But the doctors and magicians were helpless. He died shortly thereafter on retreat back to Macedonia.

The legend says he asked to be taken to his funeral pyre with his hands sticking out from under the covered funeral stretcher so people could see that even Alexander the Great had to leave the world with empty hands.

Our task in this world, in my opinion, is a spiritual and not a material one. Finding a true Master or 'Guide' to teach us to accept our destiny cheerfully is surely a holy task. Being able to remain in balance, leading a happy and full life and still not being totally absorbed by life, seems to be our real task as far as I'm concerned. Everyone will make their own decisions and draw their own conclusions.

The Slanderer - the Well Wisher

"The slanderer is dear to me,
Dear as my own life;
Without any wages,
He carries my load.

Says Kabir: All praise
To the slanderer
For he sinks himself
But helps devotees
To be ferried across."

Kabir, *Kabir, The Weaver of God's Name*

Next of Kin
Further advantages of the Bach Flower Remedies

It's terrible to lose family or friends. We lose them because our partners or family can't stands them or the other way around. They move or we move. Sometimes sickness and death takes them. The emotional and mental stress of this loss can be very traumatic. Especially if there's serious sickness or death.

However, the stress can be just as traumatic for some people without things going that far. Hearing that a friend is sick or hearing that their parents have died, for example, can still trigger all kinds of negative emotions in us. Fear, guilt, anger, uncertainty are just a few I could name. Since sickness really begins with those negative moods, it's not so strange to see how people involved in divorce, job change, moving, serious or sudden sickness or danger to themselves or to those they love could set off a whole chain reaction of sicknesses.

Not only the person who is injured or sick suffers but their families and friends and even witnesses to these situations can be victims of problems that can go on for years without there ever being a real visible link made between the two occurrences. It's not uncommon for victims of crime, car-crashes, divorce, etc. to suddenly become ill with an array of sicknesses and problems from hernia's to alcoholism.

One of the beauties of the Bach Flower Remedies is that families that would normally have to suffer with their loved-ones can be helped. This will make the problem much less traumatic and relieve the victim of unnecessary worry or guilt because of the effects of their problems on the rest of the family, thereby helping to speed their recovery.

Much fear or pain will be avoided before it can get the chance to filter down from the mental or emotional plane to influence our physical health. Complexes can be avoided before they can become deeply seated. *"Once bitten, twice shy"* goes the expression and it's true. Many millions of people suffer because they are emotionally unable to forget some terrible feeling or experience of earlier years. Even when these feelings turn out to have no basis, in fact, they continue to affect and influence our lives and relationships in a negative and often unconscious way.

Think of what it could mean if many war veterans or victims could quickly and permanently forget the horrors of the past and regain their balance in life. Refugees, victims of rape or other crimes etc. develop many and varied physical illnesses besides the obvious mental and emotional ones.

Psychiatrists call it *"survivors syndrome"*. People who've survived tragedies often feel guilty for their 'luck' and happiness. Years of analyzing and talking don't help but I've cured it fast and safe many times with the Bach Flowers. People who'd survived the German and Japanese concentrations-camps and many other examples causing inferiority-complexes, inability to trust, nightmares, insomnia and a list of physical problems. They disappear when given the right combination of flowers. They still know it happened but it doesn't touch them anymore.

Often over-shadowed by what seems to be far greater or important healings these *"improvement"* are often the source of untold human grief. They are the reason why millions of people spend unsuccessful years in therapy. Please don't underestimate the power of the flower and the help they could bring to untold numbers of people daily suffering these invisible wounds.

Next of Kin - Resistance

This morning I spoke with one of my clients who's been taking the flowers for about 8 months. When she heard about someone who'd healed from a very serious sickness in about two weeks she was very upset. She asked me why some people heal so quickly and easily and some don't.

Of course, what she meant was, why she wasn't healed yet. Her mother had degraded her and her brothers and sisters their whole lives. They were neglected or tormented by their mother constantly. This client is up to her eyes in the poison of hate.

Hate for her mother and bitterness towards almost everyone including herself. She's never had a serious relationship and never wanted one. She and her brothers and sisters all suffer from deep inferiority complexes along with deep rooted guilt feelings.

As so many children who've been mistreated, they blame themselves and were convinced they must have done something wrong to deserve being treated like that by someone they loved. None of them have any real self-confidence in spite of the good jobs and material success all of them enjoyed before retirement. Although she was brought up to be very religious she hated priests and God. Both had attacked or deserted her, she felt, and she hated both of them equally.

Finally, because of serious back-problems and deafness in one ear (because of a hole in her eardrum), she was forced to retire early. She was very bitter that her career in the medical profession was cut short by sickness and pain. Her sister was often sick and she cared for her without complaint or thinking of herself. However, she was never thanked or appreciated by her sister for her trouble. Many times she wanted to say no to her sister but didn't dare. She could never say 'no' to anyone which gave her more guilt and inferiority feelings than ever.

The sisters were bitter towards the world and each other. She was always afraid of everything. She didn't dare to call on the phone or speak up for herself. Her mother was constantly on her mind although she'd been dead for years. The bad memories haunted her.

Her stomach was always upset or hurting and she could hardly eat. In spite of this she got fatter and fatter. This was her situation when she came to me. X-rays showed 'permanent' damage to her vertebrae and several specialists with whom she'd worked said she'd never be healed or be without pain. After three months and as many consultations she was very changed. Her back pain had completely disappeared.

The pain and bitterness of the past was still present but in a much less controlling way. Fear of her sister becoming sick or dying was also much less and she'd told her sister she didn't want to always talk about their horrible youth and mother all the time. Shortly after that her sister became sick again.

The flowers were recommended but her sister thought it was ridiculous and refused. She'd seen how much better her sister had improved physically and emotionally and even though she couldn't explain how it was otherwise possible she insisted it couldn't be the flowers. Not only did she refuse to talk to me or believe her sister about the flowers she said her sister wasn't as sweet and understanding or as caring as before.

Their contact was no longer the same. I was ecstatic but my client was troubled and felt guilty. Not living in the past frightened her. It made her uneasy not to hear her mothers' degrading attacks in her head everyday. This new-found self-confidence had caused tension between her and her sister and others which she didn't have when she did what everyone wanted without complaining.

Happiness and guilt, traumatic fear and self-liberation rise and fall in quick succession like waves in a rough sea. Was I a devil or an angel? Were the flowers a blessing or a curse? She wasn't sure. She'd have to get used to a new personality if she wanted to heal. I used acupressure and reflex-massage a few times. Right about that time her hearing came back!

Incredible as it seems, I've healed many deaf people of all ages and causes with the flowers and massage. Some were deaf due to diseases, some after falling or being hit in some way, some because of mistakes from doctors or wrong medication and some were deaf because of emotional or psychological reasons.

With the exception of these psychological causes the other cases of deafness all had visible medical reasons and concrete medical evidence of their deafness but still they were healed. Personally, healing deafness caused by psychosomatic reasons is just as difficult as those due to physical causes.

This woman was pleased but so shocked that she stopped immediately with the treatment. If she changed too much she'd have no one left, she thought. Better to stay sick in a known world than be healed and face a new one. I pleaded with her to fight and remember how it used to feel to be afraid to open her mouth or say 'no'. Making a phone-call was so difficult, she'd have bouts of hysterical panic before she dared to pick up the receiver and now she'd called without any trouble at all. It was only when I reminded her of it that she realized the phone-calls weren't frightening anymore. She returned to treatment.

The pain in her shoulder and hip are still there but her stomach-trouble is over, she hears again, her back doesn't hurt anymore, she's forgiven her mother and hardly ever thinks about her. She no longer lives in the past.

When her sister decided on *'exploratory surgery'* she told her she'd have to hire a nurse because she was just too tired to care for her anymore and she wanted some time for herself. Her sister called her much less after that and when she did she wasn't as friendly as before but she was more respectful.

Scared Stiff

The Christian tradition contains many beautiful and truthful elements but as it is taught to us this beauty is often twisted into ugly elements of discord, prejudice and guilt. There is so much emphasis on the negative and on the question of guilt that brotherly love is difficult to find.

Without the concepts of reincarnation and karma it's difficult to see God as a loving and forgiving entity. At the same time, our physical and emotional health depends upon our own inner peace and harmony with our brothers and sisters and nature. Seeing the world, nature and our fellow human beings as enemies or competition give feelings of anything but brotherly love. Hate and fear can only be overcome and eradicated by cultivating its opposite: love. The strength to forgive ourselves and others is not possible without love. Health is not possible without forgiveness. The circle is complete.

It's not so much a Christian virtue or a Moslem or Buddhistic one as a law of nature. It's a question of personal survival as well as a Spiritual Truth. Fear and uncertainty, jealousy, hate, exaggerated attachment to things and people are a result of a lack of faith and love for God, our Creator. Every second we feed these lower emotions and ideas the door of our immunity system is opened to bacteria and sickness. The messengers of unhappiness and death are not only allowed into the temple of our minds and bodies but they are often welcomed and protected by our own misguided, arrogant minds.

While shopping at the supermarket. I kept running into a nice lady who happened to be paralyzed on the whole right side of her body. She'd had some kind of brain-fever as an infant of four months and had been frequently operated on. Unfortunately, something went wrong and mistakes were made so a second operation was necessary and so on. After six operations she was paralyzed on one side as if someone had drawn a line through the middle of her body. The right hand and foot were curled up in a little hard ball that never moved or felt anything. The eye and mouth on that side drooped in a unhappy way. She had burned herself badly while taking a shower once because the hot water was on the right side of her body and she hadn't felt anything. Luckily, her sense of smell worked properly. There was no sense of pain or pleasure, hot or cold on that side of her body. It was very cold and stiff. She had to be frequently massaged, especially in the cold winter months.

In spite of all or maybe because of it all, she was a very good student and hard worker. She became a social worker and even a department chief, which she didn't hesitate to proudly tell every stranger who didn't move fast enough. Naturally, with her handicap or challenges, the compliments and admiration fell like rain. These compliments were lapped up like thirsty desert animals after a thunderstorm and I could understand it.

She had been married and divorced. Her divorce was ugly, like most divorces. Years later, the hate for her 'ex' was still very fresh in her mind. It was the dominating factor in her life and controlled her thinking day and night.

I offered to treat her free of charge if she would only try the flowers and my massage-techniques. Nobody could be cured of such terrible and difficult problems she told me but I was welcome to try. I was sure our contact would be short and stormy but who knows how much we'd be able to reach in that time.

About 2 weeks later she called me in half euphoria and half rage state. Feeling on her right side had began to come back. Hot and cold, the texture of the clothes she wore, things she'd never felt before on that side of her body felt suddenly 'alive'. Neither of us could believe it but still I had a bad feeling about it all.

In our consultations I tried to make her understand that hatred was poisonous for her. She could be proud of her achievements as a physically challenged person but healing would be the biggest challenge to be proud of.

The physiotherapist was very impressed with her progress. Everything was much more flexible.

Still, she began to cancel her appointments with me and finally she called and said that she would like to continue with my massages but didn't want anymore consultation talks or flowers. The hatred and revenge she felt for her ex-husband was beginning to *'fade'* and she didn't want that.

When I told her that that was precisely what was needed for her to heal, she said she didn't care and wasn't sure if it was true anyway. She'd read quite a bit on the subject and thought I was exaggerating. The hate for her ex was well deserved and she didn't want to let it go or give him the satisfaction.

She also told me that she didn't want the flowers anymore because it made her think weird thoughts; *"why am I here?, what is the purpose of life, who am I ..."* and more along that line. I told her that these questions are the bases of spirituality and a good thing, not weird. I thought it weird that she'd never asked herself those questions before. But she didn't like it and after I told her that giving half a therapy or half a healing was not my style our paths went different directions.

A month or so later I ran into her in the supermarket. She looked at me guilty and told me that the feeling in her right side had disappeared again. I didn't want to say anything but she knew what I was thinking. She turned away and began telling a stranger at the vegetable-counter how difficult it was to peal vegetables and fruits with only one good hand but she did it everyday. The woman looked at her with admiration.

"Lord You don't have to move the mountain;
just give me the strength to climb..."

Afro American Gospel Song

"I'm Not Clean ... I've Been Raped..."
- Guilt -

The form or symptom of the illness is sometimes directly related to the guilt feeling and sometimes it's much more subtle.

A middle-aged woman who had had a long history of infections of the uterus and related problems came to see me. There was a plausible medical explanation but I felt there was a question of guilt involved.

After two difficult consultations the full story began to surface. She'd been raped as a young woman and out of guilt, shame and fear, she'd never told anyone. She hated herself and her body. It wasn't chance that the sickness she developed was related to the sexual organs. I'm not saying everyone who has problems with their sexual organs are rape-victims or victims of sexual abuse. Not every sexually abused person develops a problem with their sexual organs either but very often the symptom is connected with the cause. That's why I can never agree with these *'pigeon-hole'* books that say eye-problems are always because we don't want to see something etc.

This particular woman was suffering from guilt and shame because of a sexual crime committed against her years earlier. Even after a hysterectomy the problems continued in one way or another. She felt ashamed and unclean. Operations and drugs can't cure the problems of the mind and the soul. After six and a half months of taking the flowers the shame and guilt feelings had disappeared. So had the infections etc. The symptoms from the operation itself, namely the sagging down of the bladder, intestines and so forth plus the many mental and emotional problems resulting from the often over-looked damage to the hormonal system all disappeared.

Also there is the hidden danger of the *"I'm no longer a whole woman"* syndrome which often destroys the sex-life and seriously threatens the relationship and self-esteem. Fortunately, with proper use of the Bach Flowers, these problems can also be cured once and for all as in the case with this woman.

The side-effects of the operation, including *"I'm not a whole woman"*-syndrome had completely disappeared. Instead of aging much faster which usually happens after such an operation, everyone, including her specialist, was surprised that she was looking younger and feeling quite fit again.

It appears that 99% of the hysterectomy operations in the U.S. are not performed because of cancer or life-threatening causes but because of menstruation pain or other problems for which specialists and therapists have no answer. After years of taking hormones and drugs, talking, role-playing, beating pillows that represent the hated perpetrators, etc. many of the victims of abuse or crime are usually not much further than years before. However, with the Bach flowers, we've cured even the most serious and terrible wounds imaginable.

Not every single person is better than their old self within 3 weeks or 3 months. Still, the miracle is just as great even if it takes 3 years. As long as you can see and feel progress. Time doesn't matter. Many of these operations could be avoided and many of these women and their families could be saved with the help of the flowers.

Cure the guilt of being sick or of being a victim. Dissolve shame of surviving while others did not. Wash that unclean feeling of being raped away completely.

Hearing about a loved-one being raped or robbed can be disastrous for some people. Telling victims they'll never feel the same about themselves or that their bodies or possessions have somehow been contaminated or stained for life doesn't help the victim in any way, shape or form. The feeling of not being a

good partner or parent, or having had an abortion or *'not knowing the father of your child'* or a suicide or, or, or....
I've treated woman for all these problems in just the last two weeks. Most of them will be completely healthy and happy again soon. Without the Bach flowers, most of them have no hope of ever being cured of their pain, negative feelings and destroyed self-esteem.

People often think I'm being unrealistic. I'm not. I've cured these problems in greater of lesser proportions for almost 20 years. Sometimes incredibly fast; from 3 days to 3 months. Sometimes 6 months to a year and occasionally longer. It's not in my hands to decide how fast the healing will take place but do know and have seen that they do take place.
I can only guarantee to do my best and leave the rest in the **Hands of the Lord.**

"I want to prove to Hindus and Moslems alike that the only devils walking around here are in our own hearts and that's where they ought to be fought."

Mahatma Ghandi

Dealing with guilt, building understanding and compassion

A young woman had a very serious case of lactose-intolerance. Whenever she drank milk or dairy products, she had an immediate reaction. Swollen stomach, pain in the abdomen and nausea.

During her first consultation we discussed when this began and her feelings over the childhood home. Her mother was very critical and rather cold and analytical. The mother had never known much warmth or love in her youth and this was passed on. My client remembered a couple of episodes when her Mom had let her down rather hard without ever having known why. She had always felt she'd done something wrong.

These guilt feelings and a very definite critical and bitter attitude were the chief cause of the lactose problem, I thought. Bad skin and hormone problems made her very self conscious and again self critical. Her menstruation came every 3-4 months and was regular only when she took the pill. She works in the medical profession and as such knew all the latest medical terms and treatments and was very skeptical.

After we'd cured her aggressive, panic-stricken cat she found in an animal shelter she thought the flowers were worth a try.

Within 3 months she could eat ice-cream, cheese and milk-products without any problem at all. The *'lactose'*-portion was going well but the *'intolerance'*-part still had to be treated. I've advised her to continue because the menstruation wasn't what it should have been.

Although she'd deny it every time we spoke, I still found her very bitter and hard in her opinions of other people. She's also very easily insulted. When speaking of her mother, for example, she'd angrily tell how her mother complained about everything but didn't 'want' to change her character or situation.

I suggested that it wasn't a question of not *'wanting to change'* but rather her mother *'wasn't able to change'*. In the beginning she was irritated with me but later, when we talked about karma and destiny and her mothers' past things became clearer.

Her mother didn't have the power to change her life or character. Although her mother saw the need for change it wasn't in her power to do so, otherwise she would have done it long ago. It had to be her time and she had to have the ways and means.

I spoke to the daughter about a month later and although the mother was the same complaining person etc. the daughter was less bothered and irritated by it all. She felt no need to make comments on her mothers' behavior or opinions anymore.

In fact, she felt more understanding, compassion and pity for her mother. She realized her mother had sacrificed almost all of her own youth in caring for her younger brothers and sisters when their mother became ill. The mother married young and lived most of her adult life for her husband and children. The mother felt taken for granted and unappreciated and this made her bitter although she had no regrets for her sacrifices. The daughter seemed to understand this and she said she respected her mother more than ever before and they'd never been so close.

"I'll ask my husband if I can Hear"

This woman was a therapist with many customers.

She'd read an interview with me and a number of my *'miracle cures'*. She'd read all the books from Dr. Bach, of course, but she still found it difficult to believe these cures were possible. In spite of her years of experience she'd never had a *'miracle cure'* herself or even heard of one from others who were also 'Bach Therapists'. Anyone with a good insight into people should experience the wonder of the flowers.

It's hard for me to understand how these people have received diplomas, use muscle-tests, pendles, etc. and still not have experienced the healings Dr. Bach and his followers are known for. I'm not the only Nature Healer or self-help user who experiences miracle healings.

Fortunately, the flowers are harmless and even if the correct flowers are not used there is no danger or damage.

This therapist was very suspicious of me and wanted to know the reason for every word I used. She constantly asked what flowers I would use for this or that. I've been through this many, many times and it usually ends in an argument. The client doesn't understand what my logic is for choosing this or that flower and they usually feel insulted and we end up debating every single point. If she thought a certain flower was necessary or good for her, I asked her to let me know and I'd use it but not the other way around. During a consultation, it's my job to cure people; not to give lessons or have debates. I have to separate these things or there wouldn't be enough hours in the day.

She came for her second consultation for flowers and contrary to my first impression she looked very rested and aware. At her first visit she'd said she had had two unsuccessful inner-ear operations and had been deaf in one ear for the last 17 years.

Also she was very worried over her daughter all the time and was often a little "*dreamy*". When I asked if anything had changed since her first consult she answered there wasn't. I asked about her hearing and she acted very surprised and said she hadn't noticed but she would "*check*" when she got home.

What was there to check? You would think that people would notice right away if something like that changed but that's often not the case. I asked if it was the right ear that was deaf and she said she didn't know! When she came to me for the first time she had no trouble knowing she was deaf in one ear. There was also no hesitation identifying which ear was deaf either!

She put a finger in her left ear and I whispered a few words which she heard very clearly. She did the same with the right ear and she also heard me very clearly!

I've experienced this so often in Holland, I was prepared for the next comment. She became very nervous and warm and said maybe she had trouble hearing from the sides - she didn't remember anymore. So I stood 6-8 feet to her right and whispered and yeah, she heard me - I stood 6-8 feet to her left and she heard me easily.

Then she said maybe it was only when sounds came from behind that she didn't hear them! So I stood behind her and it was the same. She heard me easily. It began to be a little too much for me. "*I hope you're not going to ask me to lie and on the floor in front of you?*" I asked jokingly. "*I hear equally well from both ears*" was her comment. "*Then*" I continued, "*if you hear equally well in both ears; you're either deaf in both ears or you can hear in both ears, don't you think?*" She was in a panic: "*Maybe I wasn't ever really deaf. Maybe you just said that!*" was her reply! I reminded her that she'd told me about the two unsuccessful operations, not the other way around. Suddenly, she grabbed her coat and her bottles of flowers and threw them into her bag and began to literally run to the door.

"*I'll ask my husband if I can hear and I'll call you*" were the last words I heard as the door slammed. I heard high-heeled shoes clicking very fast into the distance. The next week I received a letter from her in which she said she never treated her clients the way I treated her.

Too bad for her clients, I thought but I hoped she'd at least continue to take her flowers. Guilt and fear are very heavy burdens to carry and sometimes even heavier to drop.

"The Son of Man will come again and recompense every man according to his deeds."

Jesus Christ

"Something strange happened... I can walk"

A man, about 45 years old called during a radio-interview show I was appearing on. He asked if the flowers could help for people who were very angry and explosive.

As usual, I told him, I couldn't make any guarantees of course, but I couldn't see why not. This man had problems with the government pension fund. Through clerical problems his money would often arrive 2 to 3 months late causing serious problems with creditors.

At a certain point, this man became so frustrated he attacked someone and was sentenced to a few months in jail. When I asked if there were any physical problems he replied he was in perfect health except that he was confined to a wheel chair as a result of having had polio as a child. He found my enthusiasm over healing his *'deteriorated'* discs well-intended but unrealistic. After all, he was a social-worker and knew all the possibilities and had had the best social and medical advice and help possible.

'Post-polio syndrome' is a medically known condition which is the result of years of over-taxation of the healthy leg and spine of people who've had polio as children. No one ever recovers is what I was told and the X-rays showed... I didn't want to hear anymore. I asked to concentrate on the mental and emotional factors of his life.

He called me the next day as agreed and we spoke at length on the phone. After our talk I sent him the flowers. Three weeks later he called and calmly said he wanted to tell me something.

He was so calm it was unbelievable. He'd become the *'sweet person'* he used to be earlier he said. A bill-collector had been on the door. Instead of being rude, screaming and attacking him, he invited him in and apologized for earlier behavior and gave the man a cup of coffee!

There was more, he said... *"Something strange happened... I can walk."* HE COULD WALK! Nobody could believe it. He was a well-known figure and the whole neighborhood was shocked including himself. We couldn't wait to see each other which we did quickly. After talking and just laughing in each others faces for a long time, I offered him a seat ... he preferred to stand!

The Root of the Problem

Moving to a new place, job or coping with existing stress at home or school can easily cause headaches or even migraines just to mane a few things that could happen.

In spite of all kinds of drugs and medicines, very little can be done for these sufferers. It costs millions of dollars in medical care and lost wages and production-time. It controls and damages family life for many. Imagine all this and then think how you'd feel if on top of that the 5 o'clock news said tests show migraine patients have ... times higher chance of a stroke or tumor or...

This kind of bad news should be band for medical reasons. I'm sure a number of migraine patients became heart-patients after hearing this announcement which may or may not be accurate. Personally, I don't believe it but it may be true. Even if it is true, the deeper cause is still the stress or personality problems that caused the migraine, that caused the stroke, that caused... Get it? Cure the root and thereby cure the leaf, branch, bark, fruit etc., the entire plant becomes healthy and stays healthy.

By now you know what my answer to the problem is in any case... the Bach Flower Remedies and the Mills Video techniques.

"Don't attack or criticize yourself constantly...
that's why you have friends and family."

Lorenzo Peays-Mills

HEADACHE
"Video's"

1. Wash your
   worries away

or

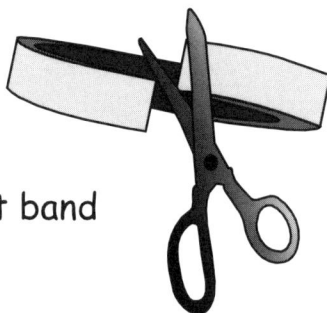

2. Cut that tight band

or...

Spider Woman B.

A young woman came to see me. She was dressed in black clothes with black military boots. Her hair was greasy and dirty. She hadn't washed in months, she said. She didn't believe in it anymore. It stifled her creativity as an artist. Under her arm she was clutching a notebook. It was her *'masterpiece'* and she really wanted me to read it.

A friend of hers had been depressed, angry and suicidal until she took the flowers for 6 months. Now she was back in school and felt better than ever. Her girlfriend had told her to come to me with her book. It was seventy pages of neatly handwritten lines. The words were joined together so tightly that a period couldn't fit between them. This was the text:

"Bananaramanamabananananaranamanaasanbatolmakaana..."

and so on. She told me that she had been working on this book for months. To avoid distraction, she and her boyfriend had painted their room completely black with a huge spider-web and spider on the ceiling.

They had "changed life into art and art into life". In accordance with this she'd changed her name to Spider B.

She asked me what I thought of her book. I read half a page and asked her what she seriously thought I would think She didn't answer. If she'd come on the advice of her friend she obviously knew something was wrong and wanted to be helped. She agreed with my assessment. I told her that I thought her book was ridiculous and I wouldn't see her again until she washed her hair and clothes. Not only that, I told her in my opinion, she should put this 'book' away and not show it to anyone unless she wanted them to think she was completely crazy.

Lastly, I told her I'd give her and her boyfriend flowers without charge but she'd have to do all these things and paint her room white before she came back or I'd be unable to help her. She took her flowers and left.

The next week she came back and we were talking for 10 minutes before I realized it was the same girl. Her hair was washed and neat and she had on clean clothes. This girl was actually pretty and was also using her normal name. She returned for talks and flowers twice more in three months.

It wasn't the same girl. There were no more problems and she'd started at the art-academy again. I ran into her several times in the next two to three years and everything was still fine. We never discussed her book again.

Memories...

The aunt of a friend of mine was visiting from abroad and had become sick. She was a registered nurse and suffered from *'spastic intestines'* which were *'chronic'* and therefor incurable according to her. The last six years she'd lost a grown child to cancer and her husband had died leaving her with many debts and 5 kids. She refused to go bankrupt as many advised her and was still working hard to pay off these debts.

The horrors of these years were with her everyday, she said. Along with this she was terrified of flying and dreaded having to take a flight in a few weeks. She was already having nightmares. Normally she'd drink herself into a steeper before take-off but even that wasn't enough to drown the fear. The first two days of her vacation were usually spoiled because of her hang-over.

In spite of her skepticism, she tried the flowers. I saw her a couple of days later and she hadn't thought about the flight at all.

She wrote about 2 months later and said that she had never thought about the hospital visits to her daughter anymore or the last months of her husbands life. She only thought about the *"good things"*. The new medicine she'd bought just before coming to visit us 2 months earlier was still unopened as she'd had no trouble with her intestines as she normally did.

Also, she wrote that her flight was absolutely wonderful and she hadn't been nervous at all. She was planning to visit her family much more often now that she enjoyed flying so much.

"For those who are sick, peace of mind and harmony with the Soul is the greatest aid to recovery. The medicine and nursing of the future will pay much more attention to the development of this within the patient than we do today when, unable to judge the progress of a case except by scientific materialistic means, we think more of the frequent taking of temperature and a number of attentions which interrupt, rather than promote, that quiet rest and relaxation of body and mind which are so essential to recovery. There is no doubt that at the very onset of, at any rate, minor ailments, if we could but get a few hours complete relaxation and in be harmony with our Higher Self, the illness would be aborted. At such moments we need to bring down into ourselves but a fraction of that calm, as symbolised by the entry of Christ into the boat during the storm on the lake of Galilee, when He ordered "Peace, be still."

Dr. Edward Bach, *'Heal Thyself'*

Special Delivery 1
"Don't call us..."

A client and her daughter, who'd been treatment by us for about a year became pregnant with her second child. Her first child had been a very difficult and painful birth. Her daughter was brain-damaged or perhaps mentally challenged is the modern term. She had never thought about it very much until she heard she became pregnant for the second time. From that moment on she was terrified for the birth of her second child.

I advised her to continue with the flowers to get rid of the fear and tension. I also advised her to use the video techniques (MVT) to help for a fast and pain-free delivery. Three times a day for ten minutes she would have to sit and visualize an exercise to create peace and quiet.

First, she would take her flowers then she'd imagine the entire inside of her lower body was coated with a super-lubricant oil. Her baby would giggle loudly and smear himself in (she assumed it was a boy).
Just as described elders in this book the baby would slide down a oil-dripping, super slippery slide laughing and having a ball. Within 20 minutes *(the baby was wearing a watch...logic has place no here)* he'd shoot out so fast his mother had to bend over quickly to catch him in mid-air before he shot away.
The doctor who'd told her the delivery would most certainly be very long and difficult would also be present. He wouldn't be able to believe his eyes. He'd stare at her and her laughing baby in astonishment and check his watch and then stare at the both of them again saying *"in only 20 minutes!"*.

My client laughs and tells the doctor she felt so good she'd make the coffee herself and vacuum the whole house before her husband came home from work...

This image has nothing to do with reality. It's only meant to be a reminder or suggestion about how we would like the mind and body to react as a result of feeling so relaxed and happy. The attempt to picture this utopian image in our mind does a great deal to relieve fear and tension that are also only a suggestion or idea about what could happen if.....

So why not make the suggestion consciously and positively? If she's able to achieve half of what she's picturing in her mind it would be considered a blessing. Plus, it gives the mind something to do besides creating terror on a daily basis as it now does.

In our *'video'* our new mother would jump out of bed with the greatest of ease with her new-born in her arms singing and laughing to make coffee. While it's cooling she vacuums the house, steadily chatting with the baby (in my videos the babies can do anything just like in cartoons). The doctor holds his hands to his head and faints dead away. Mother and baby laugh and repeat the Words of Power simultaneously:

> **The Past is Past**
> **Why? Destiny is Destiny...That's Why!**
> **My Best Is Good Enough - I Can't Do Anymore !**

A short time later the family moved to a larger house. This had been a very difficult decision which had troubled her and her husband for years. Therapists had warned that moving would probably be too disrupting for their mentally challenged daughter who wouldn't be able to adjust to a new environment. This could have very serious repercussions, she was told.

They were caught between the proverbial rock and a hard place. Although their daughter hadn't improved to the degree I'd hoped when we started with the flowers there were very definite improvements in her character. I felt they could responsibly take the risk of moving considering how much anguish their cramped living conditions caused for everyone. I reminded her that my opinion was only my personal observation and I didn't pretend to have any medical knowledge. The last word would have to be hers. Finally, they made the decision to move.

There were no problems whatsoever and the little girl seemed to improve with the added luxury of a backyard, etc.

The week she was expected to deliver she called almost in tears. The phone rang 10 times a day from friends and family asking if the baby was on the way. All these questions were driving her crazy she said. I advised her to ask everyone to wait until she or her husband called them because she needed her rest. I told her to tell everyone she didn't mind so much but she had to do it this way on my advice.

This is not entirely honest but it often meets with less resistance and it avoids endless debates and hurt feelings. To her surprise everyone understood and stopped calling.

About a week later my phone rang at 06.45 in the morning. When I heard her voice sounding so calm and normal I wasn't sure what to think so I played along like it was normal that she called at that time... she did too until I cautiously asked if there was a reason why she called so early. Then she burst out laughing and told me they had a healthy baby boy who'd been born in about twenty minutes with absolutely no pain. She'd felt the contractions but they weren't uncomfortable.

The mid-wife said there was no hurry because it would be hours before the baby came. However, under insistence she came directly, grumbly under her breath about *'young mothers'*.

The mid-wife had barely come in the door when the husband called out he could see the baby's head. *(in Holland many women have their babies in the security of their homes with little problem.)* Slowly, the mid-wife came to the bedroom grumbly this time about young fathers when she saw he was right. She delivered the baby with her coat still on. Afterwards, the mother did actually set coffee for her shaken husband and surprised mid-wife and the sceptical doctor *"who'd had to come to see it for himself"*. Jokingly, the mother said she felt good enough to vacuum too but she didn't want to blow everyone's mind. I laughingly agreed. Realizing the hour I asked when this had all happened. Her son had been born about an hour and a half earlier. I asked her please not to overdo it and we laughed long and deep. I sent extra flowers (Bach's that is) for mother, father and two children.

Another special delivery ...

An executive secretary came to us because she'd been suffering for years from migraine headaches, stress and overweight. Since her father had had a serious heart-attack a number of years earlier she lived in constant fear he would die any minute. Her girlfriend had had wonderful results with the flowers but she couldn't believe her. She and her husband ridiculed me for years. *"Lorenzo and his Destiny is Destiny-garbage"* was a standing joke for them.

Now, after trying many different medicines and therapies without results, she saw no other choice but to try the flowers. Her husband thought it was ridiculous but she had to do something. The atmosphere was very friendly but she couldn't accept the idea that her headaches were tied to emotional causes. Narrow blood vessels and other physical reasons had to be the cause according to her. There was a great deal of resistance when I told her it was necessary to worry less about her father and his health if she really wanted to get rid of the migraine.

Like most people she equated worry and love as the same thing but they are not. Worry is a poison like acid. It corrodes and eats away at the foundation of our health and happiness. It can cause a myriad of very different problems and symptoms depending on the individual.
Let this go on day after day and year after year and the damage to our immune system, for example can be unimaginable. Every time her father got a cold or took an unexpected nap in the afternoon she was in a panic. When she went on vacation with her husband she'd worry before they left and during the vacation. Always afraid that something would happen to her father when she was gone.

At a certain moment her parents began to hide information from her because they were worried that she would worry. When I pointed out that heart-patients need rest and as little stress as possible she agreed and began to realize her concern was having the opposite effect as intended on both her parents and herself! No one demanded that she be a perfect daughter, perfect wife, perfect friend, perfect mother, perfect housekeeper, perfect executive secretary... It all originated in her own mind.

In stead of admiring this drive for perfection as most people do, I said: *"Girl, it's sick, unrealistic and sad!"* She was creating problems for everyone around her. Her work-load was more than any of the other secretaries, taking on all kind of tasks she didn't *have* to do. Her boss had even asked her to relax an do a little less because the atmosphere had become too tense and he worried about her health.

Often she had migraine headaches and back problems but she never missed a day. Narrow blood vessels my ha ha! How could she be a perfect wife if she had little or no time because she was working needless over-time trying to be the perfect secretary? I asked. No answer. When she did have time for the family she'd be too tired, in pain or stressed out. Always thinking about something else, planning ahead, everything she'd still have to do, etc...

It wasn't the kind of consultation she had anticipated but she agreed to think about what I'd said and take the flowers. Also, I asked her to try to stop work at the normal time like everyone else at least two times a week and use this time solely for herself or the family.

About three weeks later she called and said everyone was shocked at her sudden change in attitude. The people at her job were stupefied she said. She'd not only left every day on time, she'd even gone home early a couple of times.

This *'free-time'*-thing was really wonderful. Now she knew what everyone was raving about. Her back hadn't hurt at all in this 3 week period and that hadn't happened in years and years. Sometimes she felt a little guilty because she didn't worry about her father very much anymore. In fact she'd even forgotten to call for a couple of days in a row.

Her parents were so used to her calling at least once a day to ask about her fathers' health, they had finally called to see if everything was all right with her. She had to be seriously ill not to call, they thought.

The headaches were much less severe, less often and didn't last as long. She was very satisfied with the progress and I was too but I didn't think she should stop yet. When she came for her next consultation, the migraine, the fear and worry for her father had disappeared and the drive for perfection in everything was gone too. She'd never felt better or healthier, she told me.

But as it often happens, people are so happy with the progress they've made, they can't believe more is possible or necessary. Don't stop working when the crab grass is 90 % cleared out of your garden or before you know it you'll have to begin all over again. However, I couldn't convince her. To prove her point, she told me that her boss had recommended her for a very exclusive management training program which had been her secret desire and objective for years but she'd declined saying she wanted to continue to have time for herself and her husband.

Her boss almost fainted from shock but he understood and admired her decision. I couldn't argue with that. She'd made her decision. Before leaving, she told me she'd just heard that she was pregnant and they were ecstatic.

Taking her flowers and doing mental exercises which we call the Mills Video Technique could help her have a pain-free delivery or at least help her delivery easier but she said she was a *'strong girl'* and delivery didn't scare her at all. It wouldn't be a problem, she assured me.

This whole episode took about 6 months.

A while later, she called to ask for help. She'd had a devastating migraine for three days. When I asked if her father was well she sounded a little insulted but answered in the negative. Not everything had to do with emotion she said.

Then I asked if her husband had been sick lately and she replied her husband had had a physical at work and they fund his blood pressure to be alarmingly low. Her husbands' blood-pressure was about 27! The doctors couldn't figure out how he could work the long hours he did as an engineer.

Also, she'd hardly slept in nights because her baby had a respiratory problem called spurious cramp. Children with this sickness have difficulty getting air. There is no cure and very little that can be done. Most often parents are advised to sit in a bathroom and run the shower as hot as possible to fill the room with steam. The children are able to breath much easier after a time in the warm, steaming atmosphere.

I've heard of many parents who have to sit up whole nights in a steam filled bathroom with their almost suffocating child. Horrible. I can't picture what a terror and uncertainty it must be. A baby in this condition and the cloud hanging above her husband was enough to cause a migraine, I thought.

After one treatment, a threatening attack of croup faded away before it had really taken hold and has never returned. That was 2 years ago. He's still doing fine.

Her husband started taking the flowers and his blood pressure was O.K. about three months later. After having talked to him a couple of times, I felt the deeper cause for his problems was the break with his father. After the death of his mother his father had broken all contact with him and his brother with no explanation. Although the brothers were both adults this break came very hard. He was filled with hate, sadness and feelings of revenge against his father.

Justified or not, I advised him to forgive his father and not poison himself and his family in this way. He'd never spoken about this to a stranger or even his wife, who told me he wasn't that type. She was astonished that he'd told me and was furthered surprised when he wrote his father telling of the birth of their son and inviting contact. The father never replied but my client seemed to be over his negative feelings for his father. It didn't occur to him anymore, he said.

About a year later we talked again. She and her husband had plans to emigrate to another country, although she was about seven months pregnant with their second child. He'd had a couple of job offers and had flown there for interviews.

He asked for and got flowers for the tension and uncertainty of the whole situation. Something was bothering his wife and it slowly emerged. In the beginning her husband had been very skeptical but his own experiences and the healing of their son had taken away all doubts from his mind.

She, on the other hand, had been more open in the beginning but when I suggested she do the M.V.T. exercises and take flowers for a pain free delivery she thought that I'd gone too far. She was disappointed that their second child wouldn't be born at home either and she would have to go to the hospital again. When I asked her if she was afraid of giving birth at home she first denied this and said she had no fear of the delivery and no reason to expect difficulties so why bother with further talks.

Besides she couldn't believe that mental and emotional tension had anything to do with child birth.

Now, the real point began to surface. The birth of their first child wasn't as easy as she had planned. The contractions began with a great deal of pain, the child was in the breach position. After about 30 hours of contractions in which the pain had enormously increased, she was in despair and exhausted.

Finally, the doctor said he wanted to give her a shot to calm her down. When she asked why she needed such a shot and not a painkiller or something else, the doctor told her that the only thing which prevented the baby from coming was her own enormous tension and unconscious fear.

"You'll see", he said, *"it'll be much easier when you can relax, you must relax..."*

It was then that she remembered my words and realized my advice had been sound. He gave her the shot and fifteen minutes later her son was born. Now she was terrified at the prospect of another delivery.

The fear wasn't totally ungrounded because her second baby was also in breach position. It was late (she was 7½ months pregnant) but it's never too late is my motto. After all, destiny is destiny.

Besides taking the flowers, I stressed the importance of the mind and the thoughts and images we feed it. It was necessary to convince the mind it was not afraid. The release of tension would allow the mind to allow the body to allow the baby to get in the proper position for delivery.

Believe me, I know how utterly crazy I sound now and how crazy I sounded then. But think about it... if tension could keep a baby from being born or make that birth slow or painful why couldn't the mind do just the opposite? I've helped in this way to achieve fast and pain free deliveries before so I do know what I'm saying, even for a woman with a baby in the breach position. If it is Gods Will it should work much better than that shot and should, in any case, be tried first. Drugs can always be used later when and if it's still necessary.

Faith or no faith, time or no time she'd have to follow my directions with dedication if we still wanted to do this great thing in such a short time. After everything that had happened she had 100 % faith and so did her husband. The basis was perfect. Every time she took her flowers I asked her to talk to her baby by name and tell him *(she said he felt like a boy)* there was nothing to be afraid of and the flowers were really a magic, quick birth oil that would turn her stomach and female organs into a golden, well lubricated slide *(logic plays no role here)*. The baby should start giggling at that point and actually see a glistening slide in front of him. He smears himself in oil and says *"Okay Mom, get ready because I'm coming in about fifteen minutes"*. The he laughingly jumps on the swing but before he slides down she must tell him to wait because he is facing the wrong way.

Then I suggested she sing the old *"Birds"*-song; *"Turn, Turn, Turn"*. She and her husband burst out laughing. Then she said she'd rather use another song, called; *"Turn around Bright Eyes"* which was more modern and one of her favorite songs which we took as a good sign.

So before the baby went down the slide feet first she started singing the *"Turn around Bright Eyes"*-song and the baby would shake his head in understanding and turn around into the fetal position and quickly start sliding and screaming *"Wheeeeeee!"*

The mother would take her flowers one last time at that moment just in time to catch the baby who would shoot out like gang-busters. The baby would then laugh and the mother would say; *"it was so fast and easy, I didn't feel a thing"*. The baby would smile at her broadly and say *"again!"*

This takes a long time to explain but the old expression is true: *"one picture is worth a thousands words"*. If you imagine this as if it were a film it only takes a few seconds. To make this work I asked that she relax in a quiet place, the same place, everyday if possible, twice a day for ten minutes.

Singing the song, SEEING the story time after time for at least 10 minutes twice a day, taking her flowers before and after the exercise. Things were going fine, plans to move had progressed a step further. Her husband had had an interesting job offer in another country. Unfortunately, the baby was still in breach position a month later.

The time came.

The contractions had already begun but she felt no discomfort so she went to her normal weekly class for breathing and gymnastic exercises for the delivery. When the teacher realized she was already dilated 2 ½ inch inches she was shocked and asked her to please leave before she had her baby there and then. She checked into the hospital the next day.

She was examined by her specialist who said everything was normal. The baby had dropped but was still in the breach position. The doctor said it was now physically impossible for the baby to turn into the normal position. There just wasn't enough room. He also asked what those drops were she kept taking. She told him Bach Flowers and he kind of smiled and said nothing.

The entire time she was singing her song *"Turn around Bright Eyes"* and taking her flowers.

The doctors and nurses couldn't understand how a woman with such contractions wasn't in bed screaming from the pain they said. She was dilated almost 4½ inches and was relaxed and happy! Not only did she feel great she insisted on going to the travel agent and booking her husbands flight for his job interview which she did! She laughed at the nurses' constant pleading to keep her in her room. Their pleads were ignored and she just took some more flowers and suggested to her husband that they go down to the cafeteria and have a cup of coffee. At this point, the doctor insisted that she had gone far enough and she must go to her room and stay there as he was afraid the baby could come any minute. She was escorted to her room.

The doctor examined her and looked up in amazement. Her husband broke out in a cold sweat. Her doctor said he'd never heard or seen such a case as this one. He went to get the ultrasound equipment to confirm his findings.

It was impossible but the baby had turned into the normal fetal position. Her specialist called another doctor and he checked her and had the same conclusion. He said he'd never seen such a thing in 20 years experience as a doctor. Once a baby had dropped down it was not possible for him (or her) to change position but this one did.

Twenty-five minutes later she delivered a healthy, beautiful son with absolutely no pain whatsoever.

Twenty four hours later she went home with her son. A birthday party had been planned for that day because it was her first son's birthday. Nobody in the family knew she had given birth and she didn't want to call off the party at such short notice so fifteen parents and children arrived as planned that very afternoon.

She laid on the couch the entire time smiling sweetly while her nurse helped with the party. She looked radiant but complained she couldn't help with the party because of a cold. When the party was over and most of the guests had gone she called the remaining family together for a surprise. The nurse brought the new-born baby down. You can imagine the shock.

There was another unexpected shock waiting for her. Now she had had the baby she realized she weighted much less than **before** she got pregnant. No one could explain it but she now weighted the same as when she was eighteen years old.

Lead with the heart and trust in God.

Lorenzo Mills

Tie the legs of the camel

Once the Prophet Mohammed was teaching his disciples about the difference between free will and the Will of God.

In the desert it was known that if you lose your camel, you lose your life. So it was the custom to tie the legs of the came at night so the couldn't get away.

One of the disciples was having trouble understanding this and asked if they should tie the legs of the camel or trust in the Will of God.

The Prophet said:

*"Tie the legs of the camel **AND** trust in God.*

You see, we must do our best and use common sense and make an effort because we usually don't know the Will of God. Even if we tie the legs of the camel that doesn't insure that the camel can't be stolen or die. It doesn't guarantee that we ourselves will live through the night. "

Nothing is in our hands. If there is a God then we must accept that He is all powerful and all knowing. Then it follows, we must accept that He knows what is best for us.

Just as a child has difficulty accepting the parents' will when the child is refused all the candy that he wants, so are we angry with God. There is only one prayer for a true lover of God:

"His Will be done".

His Will will be done anyway, so let's do our best to accept it. Your best is good enough. What more can we do?

Do your best and trust in God...

Tie the legs of the camel **AND** trust in God!

"I have Eczema, bronchitis and high blood pressure . . .

I don't call that sick, Mr. Mills"

We study the stars and everything under them but we have little or no interest or real knowledge of the thing which interests us the most . . . ourselves.

We're ignorant of how we're put together. Do we really think we're perfect? It took me a long time to get over clients who stopped treatment after they'd experienced a big improvement in a short time. I'd be angry or disappointed with them or feel I'd failed in some way.

Finally, I realized that many people don't want to be healed or feel they're not worth healing. Sometimes it is because they can't admit that they had faults that had to be cured. Be careful not to judge the situation in a personal but strictly objective way. Not *"I"* did this but *"he or she"* did this.

Science is praised in our society but we don't use scientific methods when investigating ourselves. The answer is clearly demonstrated by patient, Shelley, who suffered from bronchitis, an extreme case of eczema, intestinal troubles, menstruation-problems and high blood-pressure. Mentally, she was tortured by guilt, low self-esteem (none), self punishment and a love-hate feeling for her tyrannical mother.

After talking to her intensively, these negative feelings as well as identity feelings with her mother came to the surface. She saw clearly that it was true but at the same time couldn't' admit to having a side to herself that could hate her mother. It's understandable but if it happens so often.

The mind keeps saying if you really loved her you couldn't hate her and if you hate her you can't really love her so what kind of a dog or pig or animal are you? This conflict was tearing her apart.

There must be limitations even on limitations. Limitations on responsibility, on grief, on guilt. After just 2 consultations this patient showed tremendous improvement and I thought everything was going great until she disappeared.
A few months later we met accidentally and she said she was being treated by a doctor who said the eczema was a hormonal problem and that her mental attitude had nothing to do with it. She told me that when she heard this she was *"so happy, I almost cried"*. Almost 2 years later her eczema and other problems were the same as always. She doesn't ask about the Flowers and I don't ask her about her new medicines.

Many children are being made sick by their parents, by school or the daily news. When you got nothing, you got nothing to lose. Nothing in this world is really ours. Everything and everybody is loaned to us for a certain time, under certain circumstances and when the 'loan-time' is up they're taken away from us.
To understand and expect this makes life much easier.
We should give each other a chance and not expect that we have to be perfect.

When we take a book from the library we don't expect to keep it. We borrow it. Some books change our lives, some don't. They can be enjoyable or a bore. Whatever they are, when the time is up we bring them back or pay the fine. We don't hate or love the librarian or the author because of it.
Well, sometimes we do but it doesn't change anything.

You make me sick

The unconscious mind - which I call **no. 2** - has an unlimited power. Hidden, no.2 sees and hears everything and forgets nothing. Our feelings and thoughts are intercepted and tampered with before we get them and it never occurs to us that this could be causing a problem or that it could even be possible.

John found this out the hard way. His wife was having an affair with a friend of his at work. (some friend!) When he found out about it he completely fell to pieces.
Yet, he and his wife decided to try and save their marriage.
His wife changed jobs, thank goodness and John changed jobs with a considerable loss in pay but he felt it was worth it.

The trouble was he couldn't get that image, his wife in bed with his best friend, out of his head. It was never a question of a homosexual relationship but John missed the companionship of his friend and the fun they all had together.
He had no one to talk to *'man to man'*. Not only was his relationship with his wife tarnished but he'd lost his best friend too. A good cry or scream is wonderful in it's place.
Unfortunately, we men often feel we have to be Supermen. That's the way our mothers raised us after all.
I tried to convince John that it was natural to cry and he should do it if he wanted to. His father had always said *'men don't cry'* and for me to say that that wasn't true seemed like treason to John. The conflict was real and dangerous for John whose mental and physical health were being threatened.
The tension was unbearable. His father had cried only once to his knowledge... when Johns' mother died.

I saw my chance and asked John to try the 'M.V.T.' or visualization exercise to approach this problem. We had to take the tension off the tea pot before it exploded.

The *'video'* for John was so simple he laughed. I told him to try it and if it didn't work, to laugh.

I asked John to picture his father, condemning and angry:

"Men don't cry, and if you cry, you're not a real man and I can't have any respect for you and you can't have any respect for yourself" his father said in the video.

John had to reply: "But father, you cried when mother died, am I suppose to respect you or not?"

Then his father says: "I guess you're right. You can cry and still be a man worthy of respect".

John would see his father getting smaller and smaller until he barely reaches Johns' knees. John looks down on his father and realizes that there's no reason to be afraid of him. He still loves him but the fear is gone.

All of a sudden, John sees that his father is crying and when he asks his father why, he answers: " I feel so guilty for what I've done to you". Then they hug each other and they both cry and cry. Finally, John says the Words of Power:

1. ***Past is past***
2. ***Destiny is destiny***
3. ***Your best is good enough***

When you repeat it 3 times a day for about 10 minutes, after a week you will know it backwards and forwards. It begins to influence your thinking and feelings. It's a small price for health and peace of mind.

This video was to be repeated 3 times a day no matter how difficult or ridiculous it seemed. No matter how tired he was.

Now for the Big One, the matter with the image of his wife. After all, he wanted to forgive her everything and live happily ever after. In stead of pretending it didn't hurt, let's admit it does and do something about it is what I told my client. Only then can we start to get over it and begin to live again. That image of them in bed kept coming back... so let it....

Only now instead of ending it there John had to see them in bed and explode. Say and do all the things he really felt. He'd like to beat them both half to death...

*I recommended that he did but **only in his Video**!*

He should beat them until he couldn't anymore and then his friend would look up and say: " do you feel better now?"

When John answers that it does his friend says: "I'm glad because getting beat up, three times a day is very tiring, don't you think?"

John then says that it is and that he isn't mad anymore because "She's staying with me, anyway!"

Then he sees himself making passionate love with his wife, better then ever before.

His friend looks on and goes crazy. He says he can't take it and will never come back into John's mind again. The friend shakes Johns' hand, saying he's sorry and will miss him and leaves.

Lastly, John must ask his wife's forgiveness for neglecting her and causing her to go to his friend instead of to him.

This long story is then followed by the Words of Power.

It was then that a sub-conscious problem came to light.

John became violently sick whenever he tried to make love to his wife since the incident. Although they both did their best and wanted it to work, it didn't. Whenever he tried, all he could see was her and her friend and then he became literally sick.

The same evening he started doing his Video, he made love to his wife and was sick only afterwards but the image in his head was considerable less painful, although it kept coming back.

A couple of days later his wife called me and said John had told her everything. Guilt, fear, hate and indelible images from the past can ruin what others perceive to be a perfect life or perfect relationship. I sent her flowers (Bach's that is) and she was very grateful for the help.

She'd noticed he was a lot less distant but that he couldn't' stop crying. I advised her to let him cry until he didn't want to cry anymore and she did.

Two days later she called again and told me that things were better between them than they had been in years... except for one thing. John had made love to her and it was better than ever before, then he threw up in her face!

She'd accepted this very calmly because she'd seen the progress and because she'd felt so guilty that she was prepared to accept almost everything to save their marriage.

Now she was afraid to make love to her husband for fear he'd throw up on her again. I gave her flowers and a 'video' wherein *she saw that he threw up on her and she forgave him and said she was glad it happened because now she could say she'd paid for her mistake but it mustn't happen again.*

Secondly, I advised her to burn a stick of incense in the bedroom to cleanse it and make love anywhere **except** in the bedroom for a while.

Lastly, I advised her for the next time they make love be sure to be on top!

They're still together and happier and closer than ever before. Lies, hate, jealousy, betrayal as the ingredients for a deeper and better relationship. Where is the logic of it all?

Close the Door - The Past is Past...
Why?
Destiny is Destiny - that is why
Your best is good enough - you can't do any more than that...

"If you're not rich, you'll die . . .

A rather well-known TV personality was talking to me about the problems and tensions of fame and money. Money and a great fear of poverty were always on her mind.

I was trying to find out why, when she made an interesting statement: *"If you're not rich, you'll die in the American medical system"*. I asked what she meant. She told of the father of a girlfriend who'd had cancer and had survived only because he was able to afford certain medication and treatment that costs upwards of $ 2.000 a month.

Insurance didn't cover this particular treatment so *"if you're not rich, you'll die"*. I had to agree because someone in my family had recently been in a similar situation, fortunately, veteran's benefits covered his treatment. *"What do you do if you have cancer or need some kind of an expensive treatment that you can't pay for?"* she asked.

"You take the flowers and become a vegetarian" was my answer. She looked at me for a while and that angry, bitter look in her eyes and face faded away and she smiled in a very touching way. *"Thank God, there are flowers"*, she said. I had to agree.

'Bad Boss-video's'

See your boss ridiculous . . .

or small . . .

or both

don't be intimidated,
you're best is good enough!

That's my Boy

A young woman and her husband came to see me with a sensitive problem. They'd been trying to have a child for the last 3 years without success.

Medical examination had found some problems but nothing really serious. They had followed the advice of the specialist to the letter. They took temperatures several times a day, made love according to fixed times, dates and positions.

Nothing... but that's not surprising to me. It's more like mechanical sex than making love. Warmth and human feelings are just as important in making a child as the physical factors.

It often happens that when some couples who've tried for years to have a baby give up and decide to adopt they are often pregnant six months later. The mind controls the body.

She'd resisted taking hormones because of the side-effects which can include severe cases of depression and even suicidal tendencies, aggression, fear, apathy, eating disturbances (too much or too little), skin problems, loss of sex drive, sudden increase or decrease in weight, danger of thrombosis, heart problems etc. etc....

I advised them to stop all efforts and examinations. I told them to avoid all discussions and programs about children, child birth, fertility or anything that was close to it for a while.

I asked them to put out of sight all thermometers or fertility charts. Make love only when they wanted, how and where they wanted without regard to results.

Although he didn't believe in the flowers her husband was visibly relieved. The pressure of having to perform on demand had all but destroyed his sexual interest in his wife not to mention cooled him off considerably about having children.

I did her horoscope because I felt strongly connected to them and really wanted to give them something concrete to hold on to, to relieve the pressure.

When I told them she'd be pregnant within two weeks her husband smiled at me in that, for me familiar *"I know you were a crook"*-kind of smile- but I didn't mind. His wife was ecstatic. When I also told them some specific, personal and private things about their past on the correct dates his attitude towards me changed to a very positive one. He said he didn't believe it, couldn't understand it but had to admit it was true. I just prayed I was right.

To make a long story short, nine-and-a half months later when I went to visit my partner and new-born son, I heard a familiar voice in the room next to ours... you guessed it. Mother and son (both mothers and sons) were doing fine. The boys were born one day apart.

Birds of a feather...

A father brought his asthmatic-bronchitis son to me. The boy was about ten years old. They drove into the parking lot and stepped out but after ten minutes there was still no knock on the door so I went out. The boy was bent over gasping for air. He'd had to stop 2 or 3 times in the fifty yards from the lot to my door. He was extremely thin and pale.

It took us another ten minutes to reach the door.

His father began to explain how his son had been an avid tennis player just two years ago. Taking lessons and playing every single day as long as possible and now it took 20 minutes just to reach my front door.

I asked the boy to tell his story in his own words leaving nothing out no matter how negative or dumb it appeared to be. I also asked the father to promise that no matter what secrets came to the surface the boy wouldn't be punished, no matter what.

He agreed.

Two years ago the boys' grandfather gave him a rabbit for his birthday. That night he had his first asthma attack. The family doctor said the boy was allergic to rabbits although he'd often played with the rabbits on his grandfathers' farm without any problem. Nevertheless, the rabbit was returned the next day despite pleas and tears.

The rabbit was gone but the asthmatic attacks stayed and grew steadily worse until he could no longer attend his tennis lessons.

It reached a point where he hardly ever left the house. He was too tired to even play. He could hardly walk as I'd seen in the parking lot. In spite of this very logical explanation, I had a strange feeling there was something else.

The father reassured me that his son was telling the truth which I didn't doubt. Only I felt there was something that had caused this problem in a more subconscious or undetected way.

I asked every question about the family, friends, deaths and school I could think of but nothing seemed to have happened. The boy was open and relaxed but his father was noticeably disappointed. I asked the boy to close his eyes and relax and I did the same, then I asked him to tell me what had frightened him so terribly on his birthday two years ago.

His father wanted to deny anything had happened once again but I ignored him and closed my eyes and asked the question again.

The child answered in a frightened, hushed voice:
"there are murderers in the neighborhood. We're all going to be killed." His father was shocked.

Two years ago there had been a rash of burglaries in the neighborhood. Everyone was talking about it at that time, especially the kids. The night before his birthday and the beginning of the allergy- and asthma period, there'd been an attempted break-in at their home and the police were called.

The lock on the door was damaged but the burglars didn't get in.

The father stared at me with an open mouth. His son had broken out in a cold sweat and looked almost blue. Before his father could put the respirator to his mouth I reminded the boy this was only a story and there was no reason to be afraid of burglars or of punishment from his father no matter what the rest of the story was. I asked the father to repeat his promise loud and clear and winked at him.

He did and his son calmed down, his color returning to normal.

That incident about the murderers was by itself bad enough but when our boy told his best friend, things got hot and heavy. Kids being kids, the friend said he'd heard on the TV (not true) that people had been murdered by burglars that same night and that they usually returned to an unsuccessful job to try again. Shortly after that the grandfather arrived with the rabbit as birthday present. The father said the grandpa was the boys' idol and then it all fell into place for me.

I asked if grandpa had had any physical problems around that same time... Yes, grandpa had had an attack of bronchitis! The grandson made the unconscious association and used that as a reason to stay home. The father laughed until I asked the boy if he'd been afraid to go to school the next day and to his tennis lesson after that and he said a strong *"yeah... I was afraid to leave the house for anything. What if the burglars knew who I was and caught me or grabbed Mama while I was at school or you were at work?"*

The father stopped laughing. So the asthma resulted because of an association with grandpa coupled with a great fear which he felt he couldn't admit to anyone for one reason or another. He was terrified of leaving home. I asked if his best friend always told the truth and of course this kid was famous for his tall tales.

He was easily discredited as a star witness with no harm done. There was no reason to be afraid I said because there had been no neighbors murdered in their neighborhood (I hoped) and the father vouched for that ... thank God.

Burglars **never** return to an unsuccessful job if they're smart because the chances are too big they'll be recognized and caught. Anyone who could pull so many *'jobs'* in one neighborhood without being seen had to be smart so... He got the point.

Lastly, these burglars didn't know who his family were and didn't care. They were surely breaking into newer and better neighborhoods by now, being as smart as they were, so there was no need to be afraid anymore or to stay in the house.

The boy's color returned in seconds. His father was definitely shocked. There was no reason why he couldn't put his inhalator away, I suggested.

Again the father was shocked and wanted to object but this time I didn't have to say anything. He stopped himself halfway through his protest.

His son began to breathe deeply from his chest.

Normally he could only breathe to about half capacity. Short, jerky breaths but now he took normal but for him, deep breaths. *"There are no murderers in our neighborhood then?"* asked the boy. *"None at all",* was my reply.

Then he jumped up and ran down the steps before we could move! While we were asking how he could do that we heard the front door slam.

We looked out the window.

The boy ran full speed across the parking lot to the car and back again. His father began to beat on the window as a warning. I asked when he'd seen his son run like that. He looked at me with tears in his eyes. We went to the door and the boy was still running. He wasn't tired, pale or asthmatic.

His father asked how he could thank me. Apart from my usual fee I asked him to drive right away to grandpa's farm and pick up the boy's rabbit. The father protested that grandpa's farm was a 2 ½ hours drive from us but I said I felt the boy deserved a special reward for his openness and courage.

It was also important for him to see his father truly supported his healing. They picked up his rabbit and there was no allergic reaction or problem of any kind.

Five months later his father called to say his son was an enthusiastic tennis player again and did everything just like other kids his age. A year after that he called again to say everything was perfectly normal. The family was so happy. They asked if I knew anyone who might want some cute baby rabbits... please.

"I can't be smart, I don't have a degree"

This man came to see me after talking to a friend of his who was cured of inferiority-complexes, anxieties, migraine, menstruation pains and a hate of her *'cruel'* mother.

She took the flowers for about seven months after which it was no longer necessary. Her fears had disappeared and she was now able to love and accept herself not only in her head but in her heart where it really counts.

This man was impressed with this, so he came for consultation because he too, suffered from anxiety and very strong feelings of inferiority. In spite of being the managing director of a very large and successful international company, he was plagued with worry and fear causing, in my opinion, intestinal problems, insomnia, hyperventilation attacks twice or three times a week and a constant dread that he would soon be fired.

This had been going on for almost three years. He had tried psychiatrists, psychologists, different kinds of therapies, rest spas, yoga and various drugs (medicines) but nothing helped.

Everyone in the company had the greatest confidence in him and he did his work exceptionally well. The customers always asked for him personally and he'd brought in a number of large orders solely on the strength of his personality.

The only problem was he couldn't feel this appreciation or confidence in himself no matter what the sales figures were and no matter what his colleagues said.

He'd worked himself up the ladder from sales rep to managing director in 30 years but he had never been to college or had management training. Nowadays that hardly seemed possible.

Every new, young executive had one or more business degrees and he lived in terror he would make a fool of himself or simply be replaced by a younger man with more business education.

Of course, he knew and had heard all the sermons on experience versus education but hearing it with your ears and intellect is quite different form feeling it and believing it in your heart.

Then he said: *"I can't be smart, I don't have a degree"*.

I explained my views on destiny and he quickly agreed it had to be a 'true' philosophy because he'd experienced it in his personal life. He was business-like and agreed to try the flowers. After all, he'd seen the incredible changes in his friends and said he'd be extremely happy if he could reach 50% of what she'd done.

The flowers had an immediate effect. In the first two weeks the insomnia and spastic *'intestinal'* problems had vanished. He'd had 2 or 3 hyperventilation attacks in two weeks instead of 2-3 times a week. The business meetings had gone smoothly with no tension and he'd even cracked a few jokes. That was quite exceptional for him because he was usually very tense and afraid during the meetings. His secretary said: *"he seemed more like his old self that he had in the last few years."*

We had another consultation and he received a different combination of flowers, of course.

A month later we talked again and everything was in order. Once or twice it seemed that a hyperventilation attack was going to start but he'd taken his flowers and within a few minutes it had disappeared and never returned.

Just to be sure we continued for another month, during which everything had gone perfectly and he didn't worry about a thing. Why should he, he explained to me, he had a wonderful job that he was good at and he knew the business and customers better than anyone there, business degrees or not.

"This Kid Will Never Make It"

While treating a client of mine, I heard she and her husband were involved in a sort *'Big Brother'* -program. They had no children so this boy of thirteen received all their love and attention.

My client was a very warm woman but she was also uncertain of herself. Her husband was very closed and couldn't relate well on an emotional level which made the contact with their *'adopted'* son rather cool and difficult.

This boy had seen it all in his few years here on earth. He and his brother had been severely beaten by their father since they were about two years old; their mother was a junkie with a history of mental problems.

When this boy was about seven his mother had a mental breakdown. The father would leave the kids for days at a time which led to their eventually becoming wards of the state.

The boys knew where their father lived and even though they were permitted they never visited him anymore after a couple of disastrous weekends when they returned to the home covered with black and blue marks. This boy hated his father with a passion. He was also very suspicious of everyone.

My client complained they couldn't reach him at all after two years of contact, phone calls, outings, soccer-games and weekend-visits once a month. The boy was very aggressive and never showed any feelings or appreciation for anyone or anything except his brother.

The social worker and psychologist at the State Home had both said *"this kid will never make it."*

They couldn't get him to talk about his father or his inner feelings at all. He showed no interest in school although he was obviously intelligent. His dreams of doing something with computers seemed too high for him according to his teacher and the social worker.

During a consultation I was told she was thinking of stopping all contact with him. She couldn't take it anymore, his explosions had become more threatening and unexpected. I pleaded with her to give him another chance and give him flowers to overcome his problems. Her husband didn't agree, feeling it wasn't possible to reach him with flowers or anything else.
In spite of not wanting to try the flowers for him they decided to give it another three months. I was glad and let the subject drop trusting in destiny to decide what my next move would be. There was no point in trying to convince her husband to change his mind about the flowers without risking a backlash-effect.

Destiny acted quickly. A month or so later my client was involved in a serious accident and I was called to bring flowers for the shock and the physical injury because Bach Flowers when used properly, help existing problems heal much faster than usual. I also used foot-reflex and acupressure massage for the relief of pain and trauma. She responded exceedingly well shocking the doctors and physical therapists.

While visiting her in the hospital I met her *'adopted'* son and we hit it off immediately. His *'father'* and *'mother'* introduced him and began to tell me not to expect him to say much or show his feelings etc. I waved to them to please be quiet. I asked about his interest in computers and he began to talk and talk.... and talk ... and talk. The couldn't believe it but I'm used to this happening with adults as well as children.
When visiting hours were over we all left. We offered to bring the boy and put his bike in our car because it was pretty late and the road to the Home went through a very dark and isolated area. We put his bike in the back and my girlfriend took the wheel. He and I tried to cram into the small seat in front but it wasn't easy.

136

He laughed and joked that it might be easier if I sat on his lap instead of the other way around.

To his surprise, I agreed and hopped on his lap. I told him about clients who still had mental, emotional or physical problems because of traumas they'd had as children which they couldn't let go of emotionally. I explained how hate, no matter how justified, is still a poison for the one doing the hating.

is father and mother were both sick people.

One visibly sick, the mother more on the inside, but both equally sick and more deserving of pity than hate.

Especially since hate was so destructive to the victim who'd already suffered so much.

Why add insult to injury to another insult and more injury?

He understood. I felt his arm around my shoulder tighten as he asked if I meant him and his parents. I gave no answer. He began to tell me about the beatings and threatening phone calls from his father etc., etc.

The whole story gushed out in a very cool and controlled way. I mixed flowers for him in the driveway of the Home at nine o'clock at night and prayed.

The next day he called but I was out. He left a message on the machine asking me to call him back the next day. The day after, I called him back , he was elated and so very open that I had to double-check to make sure if it was his voice.

He'd never participated in the games at the Home with the other boys until yesterday and he told me it was great.

His social worker had come and visited with him without it being an official appointment for the very first time and noted how changed he seemed to be. They had a fine talk. This boy who'd never opened up to anyone asked help with math for the first time and counseling for a study in computer science.

His social worker was so impressed he said he'd talk to the school principal to see if this boy could enter the *'normal'* public school outside of the Home. He also asked if he, the social worker, could continue as personal mentor when the boy started at his new school. This was incredible but the icing on the cake was yet to come...

He'd asked for and gotten permission to call his father. Our young friend wanted to call and tell his father he understood, he'd had never really wanted to hurt them or desert them but because of his own problems he just couldn't help himself.
This brave and suddenly changed boy had grown up.
He didn't want to see his father or visit him because he knew his father was still sick and unfortunately, not to be trusted but he didn't hate him anymore and just wanted to let him know it.

I was amazed and sad to think of how many boys and girls in these kinds of homes need the flowers. Maybe one day it will be so. Think of the good that could be done...
for all those kids *"who'll never make it"*.

My luck has changed...

A young Moroccan man about twenty-five years old came to me for lactose intolerance or milk-allergy. If he ate fish and milk or milk products together in one meal or within a 24 hour period he'd break-out in white blotches all over. Examinations and special diets didn't help. After a long talk it came to me that his grandfather had something to do with this.

He then said he was an *'orphan'*. Although his parents had died after he'd grown up, he still considered himself an orphan because of the closeness of the family-ties. This strengthened my belief or feeling that family played a role herein.

He thought about it for a while and suddenly an old memory came to the surface. He was fishing with his grandfather who'd said it was a Moroccan habit never to drink milk with fish or terrible things would happen to your skin. Although frightened by this warning from someone with such wisdom and stature as his grandfather, the young boy couldn't resist the temptation to try it. He drank milk right after their fish-dinner and promptly broke out in white spots over his entire body.

In spite of what the specialist said, I felt it was more an emotional problem than a physical one; as I've found in so many allergy cases, especially after this conversation about his grandfather. I gave him his flowers and he promised to think about what I'd said. It might be true for other people but it would probably never work for him.

People in his village had always said he was unlucky and he agreed. He was an illegal alien, so he couldn't attend the university as he so wanted. He didn't have a permanent address or a girlfriend and these spots on his body were driving him crazy. Logic could not convince him that his *'bad luck'* was only in his head so as a last resort I took out my Tarot-cards.

According to what I had seen in the cards he'd be admitted to the university if he'd only apply.

He didn't have to worry about his *'alien'* status he'd be helped.

In spite of what he thought, everything would be completely changed within three weeks. He laughed in disbelieve.

Instead of a video-exercise, I asked him to just repeat these words as long and as often he could every day for at least three weeks: *"My luck as changed. I'm a lucky man."*

He thought I was crazy but he was desperate enough to give it a try. True to our agreement, he went to the university the next day and applied.

Of course, he couldn't get in without a residence permit but the man who had control over that department had seen this problem before and had promised himself he'd go out of his way to help the next foreigner who really wanted to attend the school. That was our friend, *'the unlucky man'.* (We heard all this later.) The director advised him to come back the next day and gave him an address where he could stay the night and called ahead for him. He stayed a week.

When he came back to see me two weeks later his skin was perfect and he'd eaten milk and fish at least twice within 24 hours to convince himself it was true.

The director had arranged that he could start school immediately and had also gotten him a soft job close to campus. He'd also take care of the residence permit too.

The house where he stayed was a student house and yes, he'd met a girl - love at first sight for both of them. He came to my door with a very broad smile on his face and I knew the whole story. I heard him say: *"My luck has changed. I'm a lucky man".* He was right.

"Just drop off the key, Lee"

If it seems like you're the biggest jerk on this green earth, don't worry. We all think like that from time to time. Often, we're right but what can you do? Mistakes are a part of life.

It's not so strange to think you hate someone you love or to think you love someone you hate. Don't compound the problem by thinking you have it in your power to control life and to decide what will succeed or fail. That's a attitude that's pumped into our heads from childhood.

We can only do our best under the circumstances and nothing more. Logic has nothing to do with it. People have been smoking for 20 years and trying for 20 years to stop without success and one day they swear they will never touch another cigarette again but they often do.

Where is this *'free will'* and *'choice'*?

Pat was like this. She'd learned never to give up if she started something. This was so deeply printed in her subconscious that she couldn't give up even on things that were destroying her.

No. 2, her subconscious, doesn't make any distinctions. Her marriage was on the rocks and she'd been trying to leave for about nine years but she always came back out of pity or guilt or a fear to admit she had a failed marriage. It's good to give up sometimes. After a month on the Flowers she called:

(**P** = Pat and **M** = Mills)

P: The flowers work, I think, I don't know what it is but I feel the difference.

M: What's the problem?

P: Jim and I are getting a divorce. What do you think?

M: It doesn't matter what I think, what do you think?

P: There's no other way. I should have seen it years ago. I'm just afraid I'll feel sorry for him and stay. I've to be hard.

M: The way of love is better. It's not his fault if you feel pity and are afraid to do what you want.

P: You go right to the point, don't you.

M: People who want to hear pretty stories or who want to heal *slowly* should go somewhere else.

P: I can't take it if he's so miserable but he never says anything.

M: Then say what you want in a letter and maybe afterwards you can use the letter as a basis of conversation. Then you don't have "to be hard" or feel guilty later. Maybe he'll try some flowers. That'll open him up.

P: The last 7 weeks I haven't been able to sleep. The doctor gave me pills but I don't want to get started on that. I'm so tired. I barely sleep. About 7 in the morning I fall asleep for a couple of hours.

M: Do you sleep in the same bed as Jim? *(her husband)*

P: Yes.

M: Does he sometimes want to do more than sleep?

P: Often, but I just can't.

M: When did you decide that it was really over? Was it about 7 weeks ago?

P: No, I told him just a couple of weeks ago.

M: But when did YOU decide, in yourself, that is was over?

P: Yeah, that was about 7 weeks ago.

M: Once you had decided you couldn't go to bed with him anymore, about the time the insomnia started.

P: That's right.

M: But Jim couldn't accept 'NO' and kept trying and you began to stay up late in the hope he was already asleep, right? It's all very simple if you know the pattern. He probably gets out of bed around 7 o'clock in the morning for work.

P: That's right, you're saying that I'm afraid?

M: Aren't you? You don't dare to close your eyes until he's out of the bed. As soon as he gets up you probably can't keep your eyes open.

P: Yes, it's true, I feel fine the whole day until about five, just before Jim comes home, then I get sleepy or get mad at him.

M: The way of love... forgive him.

He doesn't even know what it's all about. He thinks you're still in love with him so of course he thinks he still has *'rights'* and *'privileges'* or maybe there's a chance to change your mind.

The spirit of revenge is bad and makes you both sick. Don't punish your husband because you don't dare to do what you want. Explain to Jim why you can't go to bed with him. Do it with love, not hatefully, not seeking revenge or to win and I think he'll understand. He won't like it but he'll probably understand. And one more thing; sleep on the couch for the next 2 weeks, until you move out. You'd have to be Superman not want to touch that warm leg next to you in bed. So, take the pressure off Jim and sleep on the couch. It's better for both of you.

Pat took the advice and the insomnia disappeared the very same night she slept on the couch. Jim didn't want to take the flowers, he wasn't "that weak" he said but he did open up a little after he'd read the letter. He admitted he knew the relationship was over years ago but he didn't want to be the one to say it. Jim and Pat parted friends and still are.

"Troughout history the way of Truth and Love have always won over evil ... think of it... always"

Mahatma Ghandi

Menstruation Blues

In many African and Indian cultures women have no menopause problems. That the menstruation stops is regarded as a normal part of a woman's life. The period when a woman no longer can become a mother is welcomed and celebrated by the entire tribe or community as a glorious thing. The woman *'graduates'* or maybe *'promoted'* is a better word from *'mother'* to *'wise woman'*. Mid-life complaints are relatively unknown. It is looked forward to as a well earned reward not dreaded as a punishment.

Attitude is everything.
When looked upon as the beginning of the end and something to be dreaded, how can it be free of complaints? When I ask clients if they have trouble with their periods they often react with a kind of *"doesn't every woman?"*. When I say no, I tell of a client of mine...

After a few consultations with this particular client she called and said she had to rush into a store to buy tampons. I didn't understand what she meant. She was used to always having pain in the middle of her period (ovulation) and more pain before the menstruation itself.
It was a total shock that there was no pain or warning that her period would begin at that time. Once the mental and emotional problems that caused the menstrual problem were solved with the flowers she had to check the calendar to know when her period would begin.

Menstrual pain and the emotional problems that can go with it occur so frequently and is so seldom helped that most women think its *'normal'* to have these problems and abnormal not to. An upside down world. Nobody can imagine what a shock it was to me and clients who've been cured of these problems to see a leading American gynecologist on a popular TV-talk-show, declare that 70-80 % of hysterectomies performed in the USA are not because of cancer or life-threatening sicknesses or situations but because of menstruation pain or complaints. Major surgery and the disruption and destruction of a large part of what makes many women feel to be women is a tragedy.

The emotional and psychological effects of such a trauma cannot be foreseen and shouldn't be dismissed. The physical danger of an operation and the stress on the woman and her family or partner is itself often the beginning- a domino-effect of sickness, stress and sometimes estrangement and even divorce because of the ensuing emotional or sexual problems.

The human body is a perfectly balanced machine.
It has no unnecessary parts.

I can't handle it

Lora is a young college student from a rather wealthy family. Her mother is a writer and her father has his own successful business - *"I started with nothing....etc. etc.."*.

She'd been told that a young girl must always have her own source of income and must never give up once she's started something. I agree, that if a door is closed and locked, do your best to open it or you should knock to see if someone can open it. I don't believe, however, you should knock your head against it forever.

For some people, that distinctions is not so clear. Lora's papa always said; *"if you start, don't stop, no matter what the circumstances... automatic pilot"*. This can lead to some pretty serious problems in life if you take that advice too literally.

No. 2 never forgets and it's power is grossly underestimated. Lora realized in her second year of college, she'd chosen the wrong direction. She wanted to take another major but being taught never to give up, she had a dilemma.

She felt she mustn't disappoint her parents. The guilt about the 'wasted' years and money caused a greater and greater emotional problem for Lora.

She began oversleeping and missing her classes, she had infections in her eyes, insomnia, forgetfulness and finally a very painful infection on both hands. She was unable to sleep from the pain in spite of painkillers. Of course, she couldn't hold a book or go to school. You ever had that feeling you wanted to go and still you had that feeling you wanted to stay?

No.2 is a slave of the feelings and runs after every mood. Lora's mind and conscious feelings wanted to stop with the study yet they're afraid to hurt or disappoint the parents.

I gave Lora Bach Flowers and the following 'Video':

She'd see her parents at the train-station and they were both very small, they came to her knees. She'd see herself strong and peaceful. She'd pick them both up by their collars and say she understands why they think the way they do but she has her own life. Otherwise the tension causes her to become sick.

If she feels angry I told her to give them a punch and then a kiss, telling them she wants to change her study and their opinion doesn't matter to her. Then she puts them both on a train to Siberia and says the words of power:
'The past is past, destiny is destiny and my best is good enough'.
Then she must peel off the skin of her hands and see her own healthy hands appear or she see her hands simply heal in a few seconds or throw her old hands away and screw on new ones.

The next weekend she told her parents about her trouble and much to her surprise, her mother agreed with her but asked that she would give it time till the end of the year, just to be sure... Lora agreed.
Her hands improved rapidly to a certain point but refused to heal completely. I don't think they will heal until she stops with her school or accepts her destiny to go to school until the end of the year and thereby keep the support of her parents.

In this *'video-land'* everything is possible and normal if we hear if often enough. Politicians and advertisement-people know this and make use of it. We're brainwashed every day by the media. It is a good thing to make use of this in a positive and 'controlled' way and not let it happen in an unconscious, negative way.
Lora's constant worries (negative video) about school and her parents and what could happen, were the cause of the problem. Giving her a positive 'video' to eliminate her worries are the source to the cure.

I'm not trying to judge anyone, I do want to point out certain facts and I think if you'll observe yourself and the patterns of sickness and accidents, the way I do, you'll see a definite pattern. Lora doesn't take school so seriously anymore and that's a valuable improvement.

A month later she was sure of her decision to change studies and didn't want to wait until the end of the year. Her parents agreed and continued to support her. Lora's hands improved within two to three weeks along with the other problems and have never returned. She's no longer afraid to stand up for herself and is a changed person.

Destiny is destiny and your best is good enough.

Forgive & Forget

Forgive and forget are always tied together as if they're one and the same thing but they're not. One doesn't necessarily lead to the other. It's not something you can learn, either. Nobody can teach it to us. It has to be our karma, our time.

Monty Roberts, in his book *"The man Who Listens to Horses"* he tells of the advice an important teacher in his youth.

She said; *"knowledge... needs to be pulled into the brain by the student, not pushed into it by the teacher. Knowledge is not to be forced on anyone. The brain has to be malleable, and most important, hungry for that knowledge."*

If that's true of mental, book knowledge it's a 1,000 times more difficult and true of spiritual or inner knowledge.

I'm not a teacher, I'm a student who is trying and hoping to show what he's *'learned'* or rather been given.

If it helps, use it.

"Keep thinking Butch, that's what you're good at"

'Butch and the Sundance Kid' is one of my favorite movies. The two friends are perfectly suited to each other. Sundance is the man of action while Butch always has a plan.
Keep thinking Butch…

In the movie, at a certain moment, which nobody who's seen it will forget, Butch and Sundance are trapped on the ledge of a mountain by a posse, hired by the railroad owner that the two keep robbing. It's clear that the sheriff doesn't want to take them prisoner. From the top of the ledge looks like a thousand feet down. The river at the bottom of the mountain looks like a thin silver line. Suddenly, Butch has an idea . . . they'll jump.
Sundance says he'd rather fight but Butch says that they don't stand a chance against the posse and will be killed... unless they jump. Again Sundance says he'd rather fight. Butch doesn't' t understand and offers to jump first. Sundance still refuses. O.K. Butch offers Sundance to jump first but still the answer is 'no'.
Then comes the revelation: Sundance tells him he can't swim! Butch says: "*Swim?!* … The fall will probably kill you!"

So often, we're worried about how to build the second or the third story of a building and we don't even have the land yet. First, we have to survive the fall, then we'll worry about swimming. It is a sin to worry and it makes you weak and afraid. You can't think clearly and so make more mistakes and create more and bigger problems. It'll make you sick and wears you out like a lot of the cases in this book clearly demonstrate.
Worrying doesn't change or help anything or anybody. On the contrary. First, you have to survive the fall, then we'll see… Deep down, we all know this, we try not to worry but how? The Flowers enable you to do what you know you should/must do but can't. Don't worry, be happy! Your best is good enough.

"Don't look at the results.
Success or failure have no importance.
It is only your effort that counts."

Lorenzo Mills

How to play the game

It's not necessary to cut animals into pieces of shoot electricity through their bodies or separate baby-animals from their mothers in order to prove that all living beings need motherly love. Without love and care, the baby-chimp will surely turn out disturbed, afraid and probably aggressive. Still, it's frightening how many parents aren't able to give love to their children.

So many people are sick and afraid because they've grown up or are growing up without enough warmth. Parents, unable to talk or show their feelings to the ones they love because they never learned it from their parents. I've had so many women who beg, cry and command me to cure them so they can have a baby.

Then two months after the baby is born they can't wait to throw it in the arms of a baby-sitter and go back to work because they are more than *'just a mother'*.

Later, they find it strange that their child is often sick, etc. The child gets the best food, clothing and educational toys available but we need food for the soul too.

Still, how often do these mothers spend time (in a relaxed manner) with their child, really talk to the child, rub them over the head and forbid them things which are not good for them? There's no such thing as *'quality time'* in my opinion. All time is *'quality time'* and we either get enough or not. It's ridiculous to think we can pick out the *'peak'*-moments as a sort of compensation and call it *'quality time'*.

Most people must work in order to pay the bills but if you have the choice to stay home with the kids, think about it. Is career and name more important than family, than our children? If you can't afford a car, your own home or that extra vacation or child, then why try to *'achieve'* or *'earn'* it and bring down all kinds of hell on your head and those around you.

Destiny is destiny.

If it's meant for you it will come.

I'm not one of those men who think that a women's place is at home, etc. but I think women and men are happier if they use their eyes and common sense.

If children can grow in a safe, caring and as far as possible a stress-free environment by their own parents then what could be more important than that. Let's have more love and understanding for our children if we have them, and more for ourselves too. A spotlessly clean house isn't everything and we must accept that it's almost *impossible* when you have children. It just puts a lot of stress on everybody. We're not perfect and we shouldn't even try to be. Your best is good enough is the best thing you can teach them.

Be a good example!

"Parents should be particularly on guard against any desire to mold the young personality according to their own ideas or wishes, and should refrain from any undue control or demand of favors in return for their natural duty and divine privilege of being the means of helping a soul to contact the world.

Any desire for control, or wish to shape the young life for personal motives; if there is the least desire to dominate, it should be checked at the onset...

Such should be the attitude of parent to child, giving care, love and protection as far as may be needed and beneficial, yet never for one moment interfering with the natural evolution of the personality, as this must be dictated by the Soul."

Dr. Edward Bach, Heal Thyself, 1931

Many people wake up every morning thinking and feeling useless and ugly. They hate themselves. We hate ourselves and feel justified in doing so. At the same time we don't want to feel miserable or sick all the time. We can't have our cake and eat it too. Destiny is destiny. Sometimes you win, sometimes you lose. Those old sayings are often so true and hide deep and profound wisdom in them.

"It's not whether you win or lose, it's how you play the game."

We're here and we have to play the game, so let's play with our eyes open. That's more fun and healthier. Let's not take everything so personal and emotional. So many people are emotionally sick in their heads and they don't know or mean what they're saying. Why be hurt by their opinions? We all want world peace but can't forgive ourselves, our families or our friends and neighbors. Forgive yourself and others, this will help and inspire others too.

Change the world, start with yourself.

A person who can't swim shouldn't jump in deep water to save another and expect to live or be of service to another in need.

I don't care how many lists you make or how often you repeat *"I'm going to get this or that"*. If it's you're destiny to get it, you will, if it's not, you won't. The most important thing is to achieve happiness. Life is hard and temporary. The only people who're happy are those who're spiritually fulfilled and prepared. Where is this free will I'm always hearing about. Who's born of free will, who chooses their parents, brothers or sisters and family or even friends? Don't feel guilty or hopeless, destiny might save us. Do your best and leave the rest in the hands of God or destiny or luck, whatever you prefer to call it.

The Whale in the Desert

An older woman, suffering from a spiteful mother and a closed father came to me. Her own strong feelings of responsibility, a negative self image combined with a too strong love for her mother resulted in a depressed, frightened, guilty woman with phobia for cars and abdominal problems. Two operations hadn't helped and she was now addicted to her medicine which deeply increased the feelings of inferiority   what   in   their   turn, increased the problems.

I'd cured her brother who had been deaf in one ear for more than ten years - according to me - as a result of the death of their father. She couldn't believe her father's death had caused her brother to become deaf but... he could hear now in spite of what the X-rays and doctors had said.

She called one night, very late. *"I have such pain, nothing helps anymore, I haven't slept an entire night in at least 10 years. Do you think you can help me?"*

When I asked if she thought I could, she said: *"There really is a problem, I've been operated on by the best. It's not in my head."*

I told her that the doctors had already examined the body and even tried to fix it twice, within 8 weeks after the operations the problem came back, so there must be something else. I told her I was sure they'd done all they could but that they were looking in the wrong place...

'Once, there was a man who had lived all his life in the desert and he found a book about a whale.

The problem was that he couldn't read as well as he thought he could. When he came across words that he didn't understand, he assumed it must mean something he was familiar with and he refused to accept advice from the wise men in the village because they could NOT read!

Every time he came across the word **'ocean'** *which was described as being almost endless, he assumed* **'ocean'** *must be another word for* **'desert'** *which he knew.*

So one day, he set out to catch a whale in the middle of the **'ocean'** *(desert). He had the best bait you could imagine. He'd made himself an excellent fishing pole and he had determination and patience and all things which we are told make an excellent fisherman.*

He waited and waited for years and years.

It doesn't matter how much talent you have or how noble your intentions, what is looked for in the wrong place can never be found. No matter how great your intelligence or how sophisticated your machines, what is looked for in the wrong way can never be discovered.

A few more case-histories:
Little Big Woman

A couple came in for consultation. The woman was from a Indonesian background and according to custom, she was very quiet and ... for lack of a better word she was subservient.

Her friend did all the talking although the consultation was for her. She worked for the Post Office and had severe pain in the neck and shoulders which were a result of too much carrying an picking up packages and boxes according to her. The pain had been getting steadily worse for the last two years. Nothing seemed to help so when she heard me on a radio interview she thought she'd try it. However, she didn't dare to come alone so her friend accompanied her.

He told me she was afraid of everything. They'd been living together 8 years and still she'd almost never express an opinion or idea of her own. She'd automatically agree with any and everything he said or did. She had no friends outside of her family and when her friends' sister would call she'd listen quietly and politely and let herself be bullied into anything.

Menstruation was a very painful affair, often accompanied by migraine headaches which would keep her in bed at least 3-4 days of every month. Her friend had tried everything to get her to open up but nothing worked. It was like pulling teeth but I got her to say about ten words to me which shocked her friend.

In all their years together he'd never seen her so relaxed and open with anyone, including his own family! I told him to be prepared for a shock soon because she would change and he'd realize she was totally different than he thought or how she seemed. She nodded in agreement to my opinion of how she was different than she seemed and spoke a few words voluntarily. I noticed her friends' mouth was hanging open. He didn't mind, he just wanted her to be happy and be his wife and not his servant. It was no mystery to me.

We've cured these kind of problems and all kinds of variations thereof so I had no doubt, the flowers would and could do their usual miraculous work. She was glowing with hope and he was trying his best to believe. Living in fear was no life at all. Thinking everyone was smarter, stronger, prettier, bigger (*she's 4'11½"*) only made her feel guilty to have such a nice man, sweet child and nice job.

Secretly, she didn't feel she deserved any of this good fortune. She often felt depressed for no apparent reason.

God has blessed us with this simple, beautiful method of healing called the Bach Flower Remedies.

As she was leaving with her flowers, she told me she had a 7 year old daughter who was so shy the children in her class at school had never heard her voice. The daughter was so closed, she'd never dared to speak except in a whisper at school. If someone took a book or toy away from her she'd never complain or defend herself. This child had never dared to spend a night alone by her grandparents or even stay with them without one of her parents there.

They took the daughter to a psychologist once a week but there hadn't been any change or improvement after a year of weekly treatments. Thinking their daughter didn't speak because of throat or voice problems they took the advice from the psychologist and began taking their daughter to a logopedist for voice training. There was no improvement. She refused to speak or leave her mothers' side. I asked if they'd be willing to try the flowers for their daughter which they did and we agreed to a second consultation a week later.

A week later, she and her husband were in the waiting room at the agreed upon-time. I immediately saw the change. She had what I always call the *'flower glow'*.

People look like this when the flowers are working well. They look exceptionally happy; like when you're in love, had a great vacation or a wonderful sexual experience or won a lot of money. She had that look. *"You've changed already"*, I said. She stood up and smiled. Her friend wanted to come into the office with her but she resolutely stopped him and said it wasn't necessary. He was speechless.

Later, she explained why her friend was so surprised. Never in her life had she been alone in a room with a man! Never - not once with the exception of her friend until now. In spite of longer hours, her neck and shoulders were 80 % better.
The phone didn't scare her anymore. Her sister-in-law had called and they had really TALKED for the very first time. She didn't just listen - she talked and even disagreed. *"Nobody can push me around anymore"*. There were heated discussions at work when she refused to do work her colleagues should have done. This was a first.
Her friend said he didn't recognize her anymore but he liked the change. That wasn't the only thing...
Their daughter had asked to stay overnight with her grandparents for the very first time. Her father and mother were both stunned. She stayed alone for a whole day with her grandparents and they were both incredibly surprised that she had chattered constantly the whole day.
The school had called to ask what had happened to change her so drastically. For the first time in two years the other kids and the teacher had heard her normal speaking voice. This child, who had never protested or spoken had had her first conversation with the teacher and everyone could hear her.
When her mother came to pick her up, there were drawings on the wall from the class and in stead of just pointing to her own work as normal, she told a long and detailed story about her drawing, her class, her writing, etc.

The psychologist couldn't explain it but thought his work had finally born fruit. The speech-therapist sent them home and said there was nothing wrong with her daughters' throat or voice and she didn't have to come back.

For the first time, she played outside of the yard with the other kids in the neighborhood. Her father didn't have to drag her to school the next morning as usual, he could hardly keep up.

Due to her quietness and lack of participation, the school had planned to let her repeat the school year but in view of the dramatic change, she was passed to the next grade with the rest of her classmates. Just to be sure, the child continued on the flowers for 2 more months. She got better and better.

The same was true for the mother. After 2 months, the headaches, depression, fear, guilt and inferiority-feelings and all the rest were totally gone: she said she felt like her *'real self'* for the first time in her entire life.

There is no greater compliment.

"The heart is the most deceitful of all things..."

Jeremiah 17

You knew I was a Snake

'Once, there was a very rich and very lonely woman. She never had anyone to talk to or to share her good fortune with. One day she left her house and she saw a group of children playing with a snake. Not just any snake, it was a cobra!

Something happened to this woman and she felt she must help that snake and she did. She took him home and cared for him for days.

When he finally woke up, he said: "Hello, I'm feeling better now". The woman was so happy. She'd found a magic snake who could stay with her and keep her company.

For years, the snake did stay. He ate from a golden plate and slept on a silk cushion next to the old woman in her bed.

One day, the old woman woke up and said good morning to the snake and all of a sudden he bit her in the neck. "After all that I have done for you, how could you do this?" said the old woman with her last breath. "It was easy, you knew I was a snake when you brought me here" answered the snake.'

Most snakes and certainly cobras will bite if anyone gets too close. It is not personal. They will bite anyone. Cobras are poisonous, not just for the old lady but for everyone. They can't do anything about it.

The woman could have protected herself but she forgot that the snake was a snake and that snakes bite. She could have put him in a cage or take the poison-sack out or let him go or have an antidote next to her bed. When the heart speaks, the mind forgets everything. She could have done many things but she didn't. Don't take it personally if you make huge mistakes, it could cost you your health.

Destiny is destiny and your best is good enough... even if you fail! Just be sure to get up, laugh and try again when possible...

Blood... Pressure

A very worried man and his wife came to see me.

The man suffered from high blood pressure although he seemed very calm. *'Blood PRESSURE'* was my comment. There was no pressure or problems according to him. When I asked how the children were - they're all grown up- there was silence. Their youngest son had moved a few days earlier because of continued problems with the police. They had mixed feelings about seeing their son because after every visit money and other valuables were missing.

Neither he nor his wife could sleep. His wife complained of being tired and missing her family terribly. When I said the flowers could help, she insisted that she had no problems at all and left. Her husband took his flowers. His son and the fear he had was on his mind day and night.

Two weeks later we spoke again. He'd realized, or rather admitted to himself that his son was doing drugs and had offered to help him. The boy was glad it was in the open. He was sleeping fine and was not worrying or afraid for his son anymore. He had told his son he couldn't visit them unless he called first and he could no longer have total freedom of the house.

They're getting along better than they had been in years. The son has been taking the flowers for a week, we have high hopes.

Nothing new has disappeared from the house lately and a few things (not all) have even returned.

"Water, water everywhere and not a drop to drink..."

People are logical - right?
Well, maybe.
The United States is probably the richest country in the world and yet millions of American children and adults go to bed hungry every night.
Is there any way to justify this?
I don't think so.

There are many hard working people who still don't earn enough to feed themselves and their kids. Prices are just too high.
Millions of tons of grain is destroyed every year to keep prices artificially high and salaries too low for many.
Some countries dump millions of pounds of butter into the sea to keep prices high. This while children are slowly starving; not only in some third world country with an unpronounceable name but also in the USA *'Home of the Brave.'*

I personally know a man who died after an auto accident because three hospitals refused him treatment because he had no insurance. How can a government of the people and for the people allow this?
I can't find the logic. It's just dog eat dog and there's no love for the people. In the far East, people do their best to help their fellow man and animals because they believe in reincarnation and karma and in a future reward for their good deeds.
On the other hand, every rotten action will also be paid back in a future life.

Vegetables are being *'genetically engineered'* and God only knows what side-effects will appear in 5 years, as I'm sure they must. The public isn't even given a choice.
Meat will soon (or maybe already is) be *'radiated'* to kill bacteria. Cancer is going to have a field-day. What greater

reason to become a vegetarian than to want to avoid as much poison as possible in your food. God has put enough food here for all of us, there's just no will to share it. The basis of all good health is a clean body and mind.

Nature Is Perfect

Some caterpillars secrete a kind of liquid-drug which induces apathy or a kind of drunkenness in other insects. Others have amazing camouflage-techniques which make them invisible to their enemy, the ant, or other predators. 'Tank'-caterpillars have a kind of armor-plating which makes them immune to attacks. Nature have given some the power and instinct to wrap themselves up in leafs and so fool their enemies. A hole in the leaf is a handy caterpillar-trick used as an escape-hatch when danger approaches.

Ants are fooled by a spider which disguises itself to look like an ant to come unnoticed into the nest and eat its fill of larvae. The front legs are held up and moved to look like antennae and so the ants are fooled. Entrance to the ant inner sanctum is gained by caterpillars who give off a scent which ants take to be their own identification scent. The intruder is allowed to enter and eat until they drop. Ants have an amazingly complicated attack- and defense system, including scouts, guards, passwords or signals for entrance into the nest, signals for evacuation, etc.

What human technology can explain this? There is no chemist who can understand, let alone imitate or duplicate what these and other insects do automatically.

Nature is not evolving, nature is evolved and it's perfect. Ants are perfect. Their social system like those of bees and other insects is extremely complicated and perfect. There is a division of work and rank so complex and smooth working that there is no human society which can equal it.

Nature is perfect and acts in perfect unison. This can be seen again and again in any and every insect, rodent, bird, mammal, animal, plant, mineral or substance imaginable. A tree has no need of logic or thought. The insects that live in them are perfectly adjusted to it, to the surrounding area and life.

Scientific and medical law would demand that a giraffe bending over to get a drink would faint because of the rush of blood to the brain, but Nature built a valve into the neck of the giraffe which closes off the rush of blood to the brain and this prevents fainting. Now, there is no way evolution could develop such a thing no matter how many millions of years giraffes may have been fainting before that moment.

I once read that giraffes only sleep five minutes a day. There must be a perfectly good reason for this too. If scientists really wanted to learn about Nature and its animals they would get of their high horses and humbly ask the people who have lived in harmony with these animals for so long.

Why don't they ask the Indians or natives who have respected and hunted these animals for countless generations for their help? I hate to see programs about *'lovers of nature'* who shoot these animals and their young with tranquilizer-guns only to weigh and measure them.

Even worse is when they put some kind of a tracking device or transmitter around their necks or under their skins.

Then the scientist say these poor animals are just the same as before this foreign device was forced upon them. I always wonder if other animals can hear, sense or smell these tracking devices or the people who put them on.

Suggestions of using X-ray machines of laser-beams to track down smugglers or drug-dealers by *'looking through'* all of us seems to be one sure way to make *'cancer'* a household word. This would be a perfect atonement for these tormented animals who've suffered so much at the hands of science.

To know the truth behind material or physical existence we must look for answers to the non-material, metaphysical or spiritual laws which govern the physical world. We must ask guidance and help from a spiritually evolved soul to please help us in our quest. To know the lion, polar bear and eagle you can not *'track'* them from some distant laboratory or plane; you must live with them; you must *love* them.

In the same way, the only true method of conducting spiritual research is to accept the guidance of someone who has traveled that road ahead of us. Someone who knows and understands the Way. We must do research in the laboratory of our own bodies in the form of spiritual meditation, not with books or hearsay but consequent, personal experience verified by those who have gone before us. Interest in the Divine or spiritual world is possible without disregarding normal, intellectual thoughts.
There is no need to live in poverty or deny our physical, material life. We must, however, have a balance between the two and realize which is the most important. We cannot serve Mammon and God. For those who search and are granted the Grace to find it, there is such a thing as a Science of the Soul.

"The most beautiful thing we can experience is the Mysterious.
It is the source of all Art and Sciences."

Albert Einstein

Actions speak louder than words

'Once, long ago in a far away land, a merchant was traveling through a forest and he saw something very strange. A group of magic birds were talking to each other. The older bird was giving a lesson in the power of actions and examples instead of words. The merchant was amazed and very happy, for now was his chance to become a rich man. He captured one of the birds and returned home to make his fortune.

He set the bird on the terrace facing the street and went to plan how he would use this bird. In the meantime, a judge walked by and the bird said: *"Hello, judge"*. The judge thought this was a nice trick and looked for someone hiding in the bushes but there was nobody. *"How did you do that? How did you know I was a judge?"* he asked. *"Oh, you look like a judge"* answered the bird. *"You mean, I look old and mean?"* inquired the judge. *"No"* said the bird, *"you seem to be a man who respects justice"*. This bird could talk and think!

The news soon spread and the merchant became very rich and very popular. Presidents, church-leaders, businessmen and women, artists, everyone came to the bird for advise and help and she was never wrong.

One day, the bird said to the merchant; *"You have more money than you ever dreamed of and you're famous too. Can't you let me go back to my land? I miss the freedom so much and I miss my father, he's so wise"*. But the merchant was drunk on power and fame and although he wanted to let the bird go, his ego wouldn't allow it. The next day the bird became very ill and the best doctors in the land were called. *"She misses her family"* said the doctor, *"and if you don't want her to die, you'll have to take her home for a visit"*.

I could do that much thought the merchant and what could I lose? When they arrived in the forest all the birds were happy and shocked to see their friend in a cage. They called the wise old bird to speak to his daughter. *"Oh, Father, what should I do".* *"Do you remember the lesson I was teaching when this confused and greedy man captured you?"* *"Yes Father,"* answered the bird and at that moment the old bird groaned and grabbed his chest and fell from the branch ... dead.

The merchant was in panic and ran away as quickly as he could, carrying his caged bird with him. When they returned home the bird refused to talk or give advise.

This went on for a week. Finally, the bird spoke. "If I can't be free, I refuse to live any longer in this cage" and at that she grabbed her chest and groaned and fell to the ground... dead. *"Oh, what have I done?"* cried the merchant.

"The one who gave me everything, never received one moment of attention or love. I only thought of myself and my greed. If you couldn't be free in life, I'll set you free in death" and he placed the dead bird on the terrace. The merchant cried bitter tears. All of a sudden, the bird jumped up and flew into the air. *"Free, finally free"!*

"How is this possible" asked the merchant. Hate was in his eyes. *"Thank you for taking me home so I could learn this valuable lesson from my father. Imitate the Wise and free yourself from this prison".* She flew away and was never heard from again.'

Pulling teeth...

This young woman came because of tension at her work and a chronic weight problem. She'd been on a strict diet since she was nine - she was about thirty now. The demands of her work were becoming too much. The medical organization for which she worked were demanding more work to be done by fewer people in less time. A sign of the times. Naturally, she insisted the weight problem was purely physical and quoted assorted medical terms at me; none of which I understood.

This was going to be like pulling teeth, I thought. That's my term for difficulty with clients. When she stood up to leave, I noticed she was limping.

A few days before she'd had an automobile accident and had injured her knee. The cartilage in the knee had been torn and she had an appointment the next week to hear if there was an operation necessary and what kind of therapy she would need. The doctor had advised her to stay at home for a week and rest that knee to avoid possible further damage but she didn't want to get too far behind in her work. Of course, I couldn't let her just limp out...

I used acupressure massage for her knee and rubbed some flowers on it. The pain and stiffness was greatly improved immediately. I advised her to use compresses on her knee at least twice a day and to postpone any eventual operation for at least two weeks if it was possible without medical complications.

I'd never advise anyone to avoid or stop taking medicine or advise them against seeking medical attention. I do advise to take the flowers regardless of what they decide to do.

Two weeks later we spoke again and the *'teeth pulling'* began. Instead of taking her flowers spread throughout the day as advised she thought it would be just as effective to take the entire dosage at once to save time. This can do no harm fortunately but it is not meant to be taken like that or I would have advised that was my reply.

Some people have a great deal of difficulty in following a simple instruction or listening to someone else. She'd do it my way from now on was the promise. Luckily, she'd used to compress on her knee as advised. I asked about the operation and she said there wasn't going to be an operation. The specialist had taken X-rays and then calmly told her an operation wasn't necessary.

When she asked what type of therapy would be used and for how long. He replied that no therapy was necessary. *"Two weeks ago, I had torn the cartilage in my knee and would almost certainly need an operation and now I don't?"* was her question. *"Now, you don't have torn cartilage in your knee anymore"* was the answer from the specialist and then there was a long silence. Finally, she thanked him and left. I don't know if she told him she was taking flowers or not.

I was just glad for her and thankful to witness this again. *"It's a miracle, virtually no pain or stiffness"* she told me and we both laughed. We'll talk about the other problems as we continue with the flowers. You can't always get everything at once, we'll have to pull one tooth at a time.

Half a Woman. . .

This customer had a very traumatic past before she came to us. Both her breasts had been amputated because of cancer six years earlier. The shock was hidden from the public but still very much present. Even though she'd had extensive therapy she was ashamed of her body and had serious self-esteem problems.

Her sex life was almost non-existent giving huge problems with her husband. He still loved her and felt she was still attractive as a woman but she couldn't agree.

Before the cancer she'd had serious problems because of inferiority complexes and feelings of guilt and over-concern for family and friends.

It took about ten months but she was finally able to see herself through different eyes and gain a new perspective of herself and her life. Her negative self-image problem was solved and her sex life was reborn and in some ways better than ever before, she told me. She learned to stand up to her family and limit the amount of time, effort and worry she gave to the problems of her mother and four sisters and brothers which made her and her husband very happy.

"It's crazy", she said, *"after surgery I felt like half a woman but after our talks and the flowers I feel more like a whole woman than ever before in my life!"*

"Our technology has surpassed our humanity"

Albert Einstein

Sitting Bull

A man and a woman came to me. The woman did all the talking and was clearly the one in charge. There was a considerable age difference and for a long time I wasn't sure if he was her son or her husband. Fortunately, I didn't say anything but waited until it became clear.

She talked about her problems and I gave her flowers. This man, I felt, could use some self confidence... some power. His wife agreed and told one humiliating story after another about him and his failings. He looked ashamed but didn't say a word. He was visibly shocked when she began about their sex-life but remained silent. Story after story about the machos she'd known in the past and how good and experienced she was in bed. Then she dropped the big one... he was impotent. I could understand it. They hadn't *'slept together'* in over a year. Before that time he'd had no problem with sex.

I thought we could solve that problem with flowers, some consultations and good, old fashion horse sense. His wife *'consented'* and asked when they should come. I asked her to please stay out of it and told him I'd talk him only if he came alone, which he did. Later that week we talked and he said he was grateful I'd insisted his wife not come. It seemed they loved each other but she dominated him in every way and he wasn't strong enough to resist. I assured him it was necessary to their relationship that he do just that.

When they were in bed together she'd give advice or rather orders about what he should or shouldn't do. Unbelievable! She was constantly telling him how good her former lovers thought she was or she was telling him how bad or clumsy he was.

It wasn't surprising he was impotent. He'd had enough of her and being made to feel inferior. He was so afraid of failing or being ridiculed, he didn't dare to try. Impotence.

I told him he had to take his flowers AND use his common sense. His wife loved sex and needed it badly. It had been so long she'd be grateful for any effort on his part. This was the chance he'd been waiting for... the chance to shut her up for good and gain control as the man in the relationship which was what they both wanted, according to me. It sounds like some macho ape-man talk, of course but I thought she was just challenging him to be a man and stand up to her for once. He doubted.

I told him about a film I'd seen about the great spiritual leader of the Sioux, Chief Sitting Bull. He was appearing in Buffalo Bill's Wild West Show. Buffalo Bill wanted Sitting Bull to dress up as a *'wild savage'* and lead a re-enactment of Custer's last stand. Sitting Bull refused. It was degrading, he felt.
On the opening night of the Wild West Show, with President Cleveland in the audience, Chief Sitting Bull rode alone into the arena without war paint, head-dress or screaming braves. Buffalo Bill saw bankruptcy on the horizon.
Much to his surprise, the quiet, standing-room-only crowd burst into applause and screams of approval. Sitting Bull did nothing but ride slowly into the arena stopping in front of the President and then slowly ride away.

My client didn't get it at first. The fame of Sitting Bull was so great, the expectations so high he didn't have need of props or showmanship. His reputation proceeded him as the expression goes. He had only to appear and the crowd went crazy.
So was the situation of my client and his wife. She wanted it so badly he couldn't do it wrong even if he wanted to, I assumed him. Just his appearance *(in bed)* would drive her crazy.
Thereby, I advised him to tell her to keep her mouth shut about her former lovers unless she wanted to go back to one of them immediately. That was asking too much, he said but I told him to try it and remember Sitting Bull. I was sure, I told him, I saw

some Indian blood him. He took his flowers and walked proudly out the door.

A week later I was walking in town and I saw a couple of familiar faces in the distance but I didn't really recognize them until I was very close. The woman was walking with her arm through his with her head leaning on his shoulder - true love.
When I realized it was them, it was obvious to me what had happened. From ten feet away the man, my client, approached me with his hand stretched out to me with a broad smile on his face. When he stopped, he pressed my hand between the both of his. He seemed taller. He leaned over to me and whispered in my ear so that his wife couldn't hear: *"Sitting Bull ... Sitting Bull !"*.

"don't grieve over us, where doing fine!"

Death is a Part of Life

There are not many things in life as difficult to accept as the death of a loved one. This is even more so when a parent loses a child. Whether this child dies in pregnancy or adulthood has no direct correlation with the grief felt. This is a question of spiritual development and karma.

I've had a client who cried and grieved everyday for a baby who died during a pregnancy 30 years before.

I've also had clients who've cried and grieved everyday for 30 years over the death of a pet cat. Both of these people were able to relegate these traumas to the past where they belonged and truly leave all feelings of pain, grief and guilt behind after a short time on the flowers.

However, it is even more difficult to swallow when the loved one is very young or the victim of what is called a 'sense-less accident' or random violence. Especially when a loved one committed suicide which often leaves the survivors with problems of guilt, doubt, frustration, bitterness or anger.

In these various situations it becomes clear what a blessing the Bach Flowers can bestow on those who hopelessly mourn or have lost their way in the valley of the shadow of death.

The flowers can help ease the pain of such losses. The shock that comes with the news of a life-threatening sickness or accident or death can be greatly eased and in some cases this shock can be completely eliminated. After the initial shock, the confrontation with daily life begins and the enormity of the loss has to be dealt with day after day for years and years.

Long after others have taken up the thread of their own lives family and friends are expected to be over their grief after a few months or certainly after a few years. That's the theory but the practice shows that grief has no time limitations.

Once again, it is a matter of karma but we assume those who come in contact with the Bach Flowers have the Karma to be helped. Instead of years of suffering and felling alone, the flowers can very often wash the grief and suffering away in a short time.

Nobody forgets their loved ones but the negative thoughts and images accompanying those memories are no longer important and fade away. I've seen it happen many times before.

Recently, I saw an interview with a British war veteran who had suffered sickness and torture in the jungles building the Burma Railroad during World War II. This man and many like him are still suffering and being tortured fifty years later. He said:
"The tears and nightmares will last forever."
I wish I'd written down his name so I could tell him there is hope; there is a remedy to heal these open-sores of the soul.

Not long ago a 10 year old child with advanced cancer came for treatment. Unfortunately, as is often the case the parents had my number for a year but waited until the medical world had tried every kind of treatment you could think of before calling me.

There's no reason the parents couldn't have used the flowers AND their chosen medical solution without danger of disadvantages. Although I did the best I could, nothing could be done to help this child. There is always a chance and hope but it was not meant to be.

At first, I felt as if I'd failed in my responsibility and then I heard the child consoling her parents over her own approaching death. Her pain was much less and for those times when the flowers couldn't ease the pain she was able to bear this much easier. The terror she had of death disappeared and was replaced with acceptance and peace of mind. She didn't give up on life but she did see and accept her fate easier than those around her.

The flowers didn't fail, they succeeded on a much higher plane than I at first realized. The quality of her life and her death was greatly improved and this helped her and her family tremendously.

Death cannot be conquered but we can, when necessary, learn to come to terms with it. We can even, in a way of speaking... learn to live with death. *'What cannot be cured, must be endured.'*

This *'video'* is not an attempt to eliminate emotions or mourning. They have their place but is seems to me the less suffering the better. Our loved-ones wouldn't want us to be tortured by regret and pain at their death. They would not want their families to needlessly suffer for them so we use this simple image to achieve that end.

Picture your loved-one floating down from heaven on a pink cloud - smiling. A belief in God or heaven isn't necessary, it's just the image of happiness we need.

Our loved-one says they're having a ball in heaven and every time we think of them they're called back to all this misery on earth and they really wish we'd stop. Then we say we love and miss them so much but at that time we're interrupted by de deceased with a *"Yeah, yeah, but it's so great up there I have to be leaving. Just remember:* **1.The Past is Past   2.Destiny is Destiny** *and* **3.Your Best is Good Enough!** *"*

The cloud begins to rise up to heaven again. We laugh and repeat the words of power as they disappear.

People who were first crying at the thought of their dead loved-one now laugh with this image in their mind. The pain is already less. They remember the good things and no longer only the death or hospital or whatever. Repeat this *'video'* in your head at least 4 times a day for 10 minutes at a time and watch the pain disappear.

Interesting Tid-Bits . . .

White baby-rhinos walk in front of their mother.
Black baby-rhinos walk behind their mother.

Female leopards lie on their backs after mating to increase chance of fertilization. *(according to experts)*

❁

Desert toads (frogs) lay for 10 months or more under the ground or in dried mud until it rains... then they 'awaken' and 'live' for two months and reproduce.

A documented case tells of a British army officer who while under sedation, during an operation suddenly developed what looked like rope-burns on his wrists and ankles. Later, he told doctors that under narcosis he had dreamed about his childhood and the times his parents tied him to his bed every night.

The Mind is a wonderful and miraculous Machine but a machine without a power source is just a pile of junk...

184

" More people die prematurely in this country as a result of inactivity and poor diet than any other cause except smoking. "

The Surgeon General
U.S.A.

Dr. Rod Nicolson of Harvard, declares that recent evidence proves that women react differently to the same medicine as men. This would mean that what is "proof" or "scientifically proven" for men doesn't' necessarily have to be true for women or for that matter, all men. In the same way, animal activists now argue that science now realizes that results from test-mice are not necessarily the same in test-rats, etc. This means, I was told, that because of bio-chemical, hormonal and anatomical differences that test-results from lab-animals differ so greatly as to be unreliable in many cases. If this is so for animals of the same "family" how much more unreliable are these results pertaining to people, making animal testing in some cases unreliable and unnecessary.

We must pay for every life we take needlessly. Karma is karma.

The 38 Remedies:

Agrimony:
For those who hide their feelings behind a cheerful face.

Aspen:
For vague unknown feelings that cause apprehension and anxious anticipation.

Beech:
For those who find it hard to tolerate or understand other people's methods of doing things, and are therefore critical and easily irritated.

Centaury:
For those who are kind and eager to please, but find their good nature easily imposed upon and exploited by those with more dominant personalities.

Cerato:
For those who seek the reassurance of others as they do not trust their own decisions, judgment or intuition.

Cherry Plum:
For irrational thoughts and fear of the mind giving way.

Chestnut Bud:
For those who make the same mistake time and again, learning little from past experience.

Chicory:
For those inclined to impose their love on others in a selfish or possessive way, blind to their need for independence and social freedom, and who are easily hurt when snubbed.

Clematis:
For those who are dreamy, living in the future, day-dreaming, absent-minded, and need to have something to look forward to.

Crab Apple:
The cleansing remedy for those who dislike themselves or feel unclean, diseased, or ugly.

Elm:
For those who are normally confident but at times find the pressure and responsibility of life or work too much to cope with, and are then prone to undermine their confidence and become despondent.

Gentian:
For depression for any known reason. For setbacks that cause discouragement or disappointment.

Gorse:
For those who have lost hope of being well or of the subject of their hopelessness ever returning to normality. They are pessimistic and see only the negative outcome.

Heather:
For those who are in need of company and companionship. The are talkative and hold on to a person'[s attention for as long as possible whilst they go into detail about their problems or personal life.

Holly:
For hatred, envy, suspicion, revenge, jealousy - all the feelings that eat away at the love within us.

Honeysuckle:

For those whose thoughts linger in the past at the expense of their enjoyment of the present: when the mind dwells on happy memories, re-lives some unpleasant incidents or yearns for how things used to be.

Hornbeam:

For those who feel they have insufficient strength to face the day ahead, or task in hand. Those who procrastinate and put things off "until tomorrow".

Impatiens:

For those who are inclined to impatience and irritation at slowness. They want things done in a hurry and are therefor in a hurry themselves.

Larch:

For those who lack confidence in their ability: those who do not believe in themselves, are afraid of failure and so do not try.

Mimulus:

For those who are afraid and lack courage. For everyday, known fears, and for those who are shy, or timid.

Mustard:

For depression for no apparent reason. An unhappiness that descends and then lifts like a passing cloud but without an identifiable cause.

Oak:

For those who have an inner strength - the plodders who soldier on through life despite its pitfalls.

Olive:
For tiredness, fatigue, exhaustion. When one has been working hard, studying or concentrating and feels drained as a result.

Pine:
For those who feel guilty and blame themselves, even for something that was not their fault: harboring a guilt complex or have a guilty conscience from which they are unable to set themselves free.

Red Chestnut:
For those who are afraid for the safety and well-being of those they care about: over-anxious and fearful.

Rock Rose:
For terror, panic, nightmares and other fears of a horrifying nature.

Rock Water:
For those who are strict with themselves, set themselves high standards and targets and demand perfection of their efforts.

Scleranthus:
For those who are indecisive, debating the pro's and con's of every situation - hesitating "should I or shouldn't I ?"

Star of Bethlehem:
For shock, the effects of serious news, bereavement, sorrow and grief.

Sweet Chestnut:
For utter despair - heartbreaking anguish as though there is no end in sight.

Vervain:

For those who are incensed by injustice. They speak out to make their point known, try to persuade others to believe in what they have to say. They work hard, enthusiastic in all they embark upon, and are prone to become tense and highly stressed.

Vine:

For those who are of a strong and dominant nature. The leaders who are tempted to use their position and strength to control others, taking no notice of their feelings or preferences, demanding obedience and acceptance of their orders.

Walnut:

The remedy for change and any period of adjustment when one feels unsettled, and for those why are influenced or distracted by the influence of others.

Water Violet:

For those who are reserved, self-contained, dignified people who enjoy peace and quiet. May become "cut off" due to their need for privacy and may therefore appear aloof or unapproachable.

White Chestnut:

For worrying thoughts and mental arguments that interfere with rest and peace of mind.

Wild Oat:

For those who are at a cross-road in life and do knot know in which direction they should proceed. They tend to feel unfulfilled and dissatisfied with what they have achieved, and have ambitions to do something of value.

Wild Rose:

For those who are unmotivated and resigned to all that happens. Not interested in change: happy with life the way it is. For apathy and resignation or feelings of staleness.

Willow:

For resentment or bitterness. For those who find it hard to forgive and forget, but dwell on negativity and their own misfortunes.

Rescue Remedy:

A combination of Star of Bethlehem, Rock Rose, Clematis, Cherry Plum and Impatiens. The composite for emergencies - accidents, examination nerves etc. Its all-round calming properties are comforting in a crisis. Rescue Remedy can also be applied to the skin to remove the shock or minor burn. Rescue Remedy Cream (which also contains Crab Apple for its cleansing properties) is also very soothing for external application and as it is a general healing salve, can be applied to abrasions, bruises, skin irritation etc.

A few remedies can be given at a time, depending on your needs, up to about six or seven. They are quite harmless and so no overdose or conflict can occur. They can be taken quite safely with other medication, and because they are benign in their action will not interfere with other treatments you may be taking. The Remedies are however, preserved in brandy and so it is recommended that they are diluted in water as follows:
having chosen your remedies, put 2 drops of each one into a bottle of approximately 30 ml (1oz) size (a smaller bottle will do just as well if necessary). Then fill up with mineral-water (spring water without carbonation!).
Then, from this prepared bottle, take 4 drops at least 4 times daily, or more often if required.

"We identified ourselves through our strengths so we'd talk about the past all the time. I couldn't believe it, after a couple of days on the flowers my mother said 'these things out of the past aren't really important anymore. Why dredge them up?"
She was so casual, I wasn't even sure if she realized how significant this was for both of us. I wanted to scream but I didn't make a sound. I just kept thinking: is this my mother?"

A patient

From an article in "Onkruid" Sept./Oct. '95
(*Onkruid* is a Dutch magazine about alternative lifestyle)

Lorenzo and the Miracle of the Flowers

The deaf hear, the blind see and cripples walk and sicknesses like migraine headache, eczema, overweight and psychological traumas disappear.
Bach Flower-therapist, Lorenzo Mills must constantly fight against a wave of disbelief because the results are so incredible. *'Onkruid'*("WEEDS") had an exciting afternoon with this American who resides in Holland. We spoke with patients who in spite of their own disbelief were healed by the flower power of the Bach Flower Therapy.

Peace and harmony

For hundreds of people is Lorenzo's Bach therapy their last chance. Most of them have already passed all the different stages of the medical industry, from operation to aggressive hormone-cures and other medical treatments.
They also have made the long journey by clairvoyants, healers, hypnotists and nature-healers. Eventually, they appear in the apartment in Den Bosch where Lorenzo has his practice. In the living-room annex work space are a couple of chairs, a table and a personal computer.
The phone rings repeatedly.
The 'flowers' are the cornerstone of Lorenzo's practice but acupressure-massage and astrology are also important aspects of the American's work.
"When peace and harmony come to a person, health and strength will return in the body." That these words from Dr.

Edward Bach are no fantasies of a daydreamer but an absolute truth is part of Lorenzo's daily routine.

"People will just be more comfortable with themselves and feel better as a result." says the American.

Are we dealing with a dreamer?

Lorenzo is constantly being confronted with disbelief. The in California born and raised flower-therapist/writer, has been living in Holland since 1973 and speaks our language surprisingly well. *"This is all fantasy"* said some of the Dutch publishers.

Often skeptics say: *"if it's true, why haven't we heard about it on TV."* The world should know about this. But here, again, the same problem: people just don't believe it!

The editorial board of *'Onkruid'* magazine also had its doubts about these wonder-healings. That with the Bach flowers you could transgress negative emotions into the opposite, they could imagine. But that the flowers could also be a source of wondrous healing? To me the task to see if we were dealing with a dreamer or not. But while interviewing the healed patients, my skepticism disappears little by little.

The serious intestinal problems from the little son of Mrs..., disappeared like snow in the sun. *"Our other son was also deeply impressed,'* she tells. *"He has diabetes, an illness that according to Lorenzo can also be cured with the flowers. But he doesn't believe in it. Very strange of course. The results with our youngest son were so tangible. But of course, we can't force anybody to be healed."*

That nobody believes Lorenzo Mills comes up several times throughout an enervating conversation which lasts for three hours and in which he confirms what his clients told me.

Lorenzo Mills is flowing over with enthusiasm. At the same time he also spreads a sea of peace.

"You tell everything to Lorenzo," says a migraine-patient for years but since may 1994 healed with Lorenzo's Bach Flowers. *"Lorenzo has something special. Most specialists hardly look at you but Lorenzo looks right through you with his whole attitude and wisdom,"* agrees a man who was heavily injured on his knee and can now, thanks to the flower-therapy, walk and even ride the bicycle normally.

"I am not afraid, I am skeptical"

"This man was 80 % deaf," tells Lorenzo.

"When I massaged him, he managed to hear and repeat the last words I said. His 16 year old daughter was there too. She started shaking and wanted to leave immediately. I am not afraid, she said, I am skeptical. That's okay, I said, but there's a difference between being skeptical and being blind. Your father can hear again, that's the proof".

This man himself, couldn't believe it either. I told him to take the hearing-aid out for a few hours every day and build it up slowly. At a certain moment he called me and says he didn't dare to take his hearing-aid out! *"I hear too much"*, he said. I said, *"Your body is healed but your mind is still lagging behind."*

She temporarily saw five or six times

"In all these years there have been two patients who stand out in my mind because they stopped with the flowers because they or their family couldn't deal with the healing. A blind woman was one of these people. She took the drops consistently for a year and a half. She saw temporarily five or six times but she was living in an extremely difficult family-situation.

There was enormous hostility towards me and the flower-therapy in the family. I thought that the family didn't really want the mother to heal. They were better off with this status quo.

Sometimes, a healing isn't convenient for the closest members of the family or the partner.

Sometimes, the patient himself can't accept a healing. Daily life is often centered around the illness. Conversations, habits, eating habits, life-goals, everything is influenced by the disease.

When somebody heals in a couple of weeks, or even days, then everything has to be adapted. For some people there is too much happening in a short time.

A good example of this was a patient, a woman who was deaf in her right ear and blind her right eye. After a week with the flowers she could hear again and after two weeks she could see again. Her boyfriend, who had diabetes, called me enthusiastically. He also wanted to start therapy.

After ten days of the flowers, he had a blood-check in the hospital. He called me ecstatically to tell me the results. His blood-sugar was improved by 70%!

Because the doctors thought something had gone wrong, they did another test a couple of days later with the result that the blood-sugar wasn't improved by 70% but by 80%!

A short while later, the woman who could see and hear again with the flowers, called me. I am stopping with the flowers, she said angrily. She felt different than usual and that wasn't what she had expected or wanted!

Three weeks later, she was deaf again. In spite of the obvious improvement. Her boyfriend stopped with the flowers right after that and in the shortest time his blood-sugar was the same as before he started on the flowers. Sad."

Words of Power

Also Lorenzo's own philosophy strengthens the healing-process of the patient.

Lorenzo gives his patients his own **'Words of Power'.**

TESTIMONIALS

From an article in "Onkruid" Sept./Oct. '95
(*Onkruid* is a Dutch magazine about alternative lifestyle)

Woman - 25 years old
Whiplash since she was 6 years old

"When I was six, I got run over by a motorbike and hit my neck on the sidewalk.
Seven years later, I got a serious form of migraine. For years I only slept for three to four hours a night.
I was tested for colleges but eventually couldn't finish high school because of sickness. In crowded rooms I would have difficulty breathing and even faint.
I saw a neurologist for six years. I took a lot of pills every day and had to take a shot of Imigrain twice a day. My hair started to fall out so I stopped and went back to the pain killer. I ate whole packages of pain-killers. Normally, I would take fifteen pills a day but on heavy days, I would double it.
I went to physiotherapists, chiropractors, paranormal healers. Nothing helped.
Out of desperation I went to see Lorenzo with a bursting headache. During the first consultation he massaged my hands with the acupressure-massage. I don't know how he did it but the pain went away immediately.
The night after the consultation I slept, for the first time in years, for seven hours without waking up. He also gave me the flower-drops. Ever since then it's been going better and better.
Now, I do things that I had never thought possible.
I paint, fix my house up, you name it."

Man - 46 years old
Deaf for the last 25 years

"On the left side, I am completely deaf, on the right side I hear for ca. 20 %. I didn't hear anything without a hearing-aid.
And now I am here, talking on the phone with you. It takes a lot of my concentration but I can hear. And then to think that I was deaf only two months ago! It's a fact, my hearing is coming back step by step on the right side. I practice every day for two hours without the hearing-aid.
Also, *with* the hearing-aid, I can hear much better. I can hear the water running from the tap, the cars driving by. My right-ear used to be very moist, but the specialist has noticed that the ear is almost clean. I've been using a hearing-aid since I was 25 years old. I had no hope that I'd ever be able to hear normally again,"

Mother of 9 year old boy
Chronic constipation

"Lorenzo's flowers relieved my boy from the terrible pains he had when going to the bathroom. Diets with a lot of fibers, daily use of suppositories and enemas could only tempo-rarely lighten the pain but couldn't cure the problem. We had to shoot liquids into the anus to improve bowel- movement but that didn't help either. This problem controlled the life of the whole family. Lorenzo lived across from us and said: Why don't you try the flowers? I'm so grateful. His symptoms disappeared within a few days and have never come back (4 years) after just two treatments."

Woman - 45 years old
Deaf in one ear because of a hole in her ear-drum (6 years)

"From 1977 to 1983, I was deaf in my right ear. It was a result of a fall from the stairs. The specialist wanted to operate on me but that wasn't without risks, they warned.

The choice between that and taking a few drops a day from Lorenzo was very easy. After only a couple of days I noticed a results. For years, I've been hearing normally as before. I come in contact with Lorenzo through family when he worked mostly with Astrology. I thought that was very interesting but I didn't really believe in it.

Lorenzo did my horoscope and predicted I would be healed and hear again and have another baby. I'd just gotten a divorce and didn't have a friend and I didn't want one.

In short: I didn't believe a word. But my new daughter is now 6 years old. Everything is so much better with me now. I used to worry about everything. I'm not interested in that all now. People just have to accept me the way I am."

Man - 67 years old
Insomnia, 50 years of war-trauma's

"I've had trouble sleeping for years. I would stay awake worrying over the shit the government and the Foundation 1940-1945 put me through. I was destroyed when I came out of the Japanese concentration camp but the civil service garbage that the Foundation stuck me with was even worse.

Whatever, as an employee of TNO (an organization of engineers and scientists who test the reliability of different product claims).

I was pretty skeptical about the Bach Flower Therapy. But I have to say, the drops have helped me quite a bit. I sleep more now and deeper and I face the world more relaxed. Nightmares and thoughts about the war and the camp have disappeared."

Woman - 46 years old
Chronic nasal-infection (for 26 years) and migraine (for 30 years), Phobia and fear

"Since I was twenty my life has been determined by my nasal-infection. Especially in the "R"-months (from September till April). I also suffered from terrible headaches. The pain so great, I often didn't dare to open my eyes. My jaws felt very heavy and with the least physical exertion they'd begin to pound. I'd lay in bed for days in the dark.

I also had phobias for sirens, elevators, thunder and even to pick up the phone. I've had countless penicillin cures and for years I took at least two packs of aspirins per week. Four of five times a year, I had to have very painful 'cleaning' of the nose and jaw cavities. I went to faith-healers but nothing helped. I went to an acupuncturist and afterwards began to limp.

The psychiatrist told me it was psycho-somatic and the social worker had me pretend my stepfather was there in an empty chair and I was supposed to talk over everything from my youth and express my anger.

Maybe he was the cause of all the trouble. It didn't help. I even got a new problem from that therapy. Every time I saw an empty chair, I thought about my stepfather and either flew into a panic or got sick.

I met Lorenzo in our cafeteria. I have been taking drops since March 1994 and the results are unbelievable.

I'm so much more relaxed and confident. I can handle life now and haven't had any more trouble with nasal-infection and the phobias have all disappeared. I even like riding in the elevator. I've become a flower."

Mother of 2 year old spastic boy

"He laughs, makes more and more contact with the outside world, cries much less, moves more and eats good.
The pediatrician, who I didn't tell about the Bach Therapy was very surprised by his sudden improvement. Two pediatricians and a physical therapist diagnosed a form of spastic sickness when he was nine months old. He was completely cramped. He pressed his arms against his body day and night. He had no contact with the outside world and showed no interest for toys.
After a telephone-consult with Lorenzo, he sent us 'flowers' and we gave him ten times a day four drops of 'flowers'.
My mother called a week later when he was staying with her for a day, crying from joy: He was laughing and playing with a toy car! Since then, he's getting better and better. I'm not the type who believes in miracles."

Mother of 2 year old boy suffering from Spurious Croup (ed. coughing, constant colds and shortness of breath)

"He had attacks of croup and shortness of breath every two weeks. It seemed like he would suffocate. He squealed like a seal. Terrifying. It always seemed to happen around midnight. As the attacks began, I turned on the hot water in the shower and put him in the steam to help him breathe. With a little luck he would feel a little better after an hour.
The doctor kept telling me it would get better as he got older but that I'd have to learn to live with it for now. Under the motto: if it doesn't help it won't hurt, I called Lorenzo for the Bach therapy. I gave my little boy his daily doses of flowers and the

attacks disappeared immediately. He's much sweeter and happier. That comes from the flowers too."

Man - approx. 40 years old
Crippled (knee) 2 unsuccessful operations

"Thanks to Lorenzo's therapy I can walk again. Nobody believes it but it's true. Our friends al-most fainted form surprise. I can easily walk an hour in the woods without any trouble. I had really given up all hope of ever walking again.

The specialist broke my leg and sawed my shin-bone in two and took a piece of the bone our to put it into my knee-cap, without my knowledge or approval. After I was in a cast for six weeks. Every four weeks X-rays were taken. Nothing helped.

I went to another hospital for a second opinion.

I was operated on my knee a second time. That whole mess took two years. I landed in disability and my limp became worse and worse. I was declared 100% disabled and told I would never be able to work again.

I met Lorenzo at a congress for psychics and he gave me some drops and in a few days I began to walk a lot better! After about a month, I could even play tennis again. I'm no longer on disability and work part-time again, ride a bike and walk without a limp. I've even forgiven the doctors their medical blunders!"

(editors note: This man has been declared 100% healthy and is now working full time again)

Man - 59 years old
Insomnia, artrosis (hardening of the arteries), war trauma

"From my sixth to my tenth year, I was in a Japanese concentration camp. Three years ago I was in the hospital for war victims, Center '40 -'45 in Oestgeest, for nine months.

They wanted me to take tranquilizers but I refused. They became very angry. Not long after that I got octrose, a kind of hardening of the arteries. I had trouble walking.

End of January I used the flowerdrops from Lorenzo. I don't feel great. The fact is that I can move a lot easier, I'm calm, sleep better and have much less trouble with nightmares."

Bibliography

Singh, Charan, Maharaj Ji; *Philosophy of the Masters, series III*, Punjab, Radha Soami Satsang, Beas. India 1965.

Singh, Charan, Maharaj Ji ; *Die to Live*, Punjab, Radha Soami Satsang, Beas. India 1979.

Singh, Charan, Maharaj Ji ; *Spiritual Heritage*, Punjab, Radha Soami Satsang, Beas. India 1983.

E.H. Whinfield ; *Teachings of Rumi*: The Masnavi VI

Brian Hines ; *God's Whisper, Creation's Thunder, Echoes of Ultimate Reality in the New Physics.* Threshold Books 1995.

J.K. Sethi ; *Kabir, The Weaver of God's Name*, Punjab, Radha Soami Satsang, Beas. India 1984.

Dr. Edward Bach ; *The Twelve Healers*, The C.W. Daniel Company Ltd., London.

Dr. Edward Bach ; *Heal Thyself*, The C.W. Daniel Company Ltd., London.

Order Form   ISBN 0-9663908-7-3 - $ 16,99³/₄

Guaranteed to change your way of thinking for the better !

Fax orders: (626) 791-6891

Telephone orders: Call Toll Free (888) 806-4557
(888) 80-MILLS

On-line orders: mills.bachflowers@wxs.nl

Postal orders: Power Flower Publishing
1885 Locust Street #561
Pasadena, CA 91107, USA

Please send ..... copy of *'MY BEST IS GOOD ENOUGH'* to:

....

....

....

....

Sales tax:
Please add 7.75 % for books shipped to California addresses.

Shipping:
Please add $ 4.00 for shipment cost for the first book and $ 2.00 for each additional book.

Payment:
O Cheque
O Credit Card: ❑ VISA, ❑ MasterCard, ❑ Optima, ❑ AMEX,
❑ Discover
Card number: ....
Name on card: .... Exp. Date: .... / ....

Call ***toll free*** and ***order now***

Order Form   ISBN 0-9663908-7-3 - $ 16,99³/₄

Guaranteed to change your way of thinking for the better !

Fax orders: (626) 791-6891

Telephone orders: Call Toll Free (888) 806-4557
(888) 80-MILLS

On-line orders: mills.bachflowers@wxs.nl

Postal orders: Power Flower Publishing
1885 Locust Street #561
Pasadena, CA 91107, USA

Please send ..... copy of *'MY BEST IS GOOD ENOUGH'* to:

....

....

....

....

Sales tax:
Please add 7.75 % for books shipped to California addresses.

Shipping:
Please add $ 4.00 for shipment cost for the first book and $ 2.00 for each additional book.

Payment:
O Cheque
O Credit Card: ❑ VISA, ❑ MasterCard, ❑ Optima, ❑ AMEX,
❑ Discover
Card number: ....
Name on card: .... Exp. Date: .... / ....

Call *toll free* and *order now*

Order Form   ISBN 0-9663908-7-3 - $ 16,99³/₄

Guaranteed to change your way of thinking for the better !

Fax orders: (626) 791-6891

Telephone orders: Call Toll Free (888) 806-4557
(888) 80-MILLS

On-line orders: mills.bachflowers@wxs.nl

Postal orders: Power Flower Publishing
1885 Locust Street #561
Pasadena, CA 91107, USA

Please send ..... copy of *'MY BEST IS GOOD ENOUGH'* to:

....

....

....

....

Sales tax:
Please add 7.75 % for books shipped to California addresses.

Shipping:
Please add $ 4.00 for shipment cost for the first book and $ 2.00 for each additional book.

Payment:
O Cheque
O Credit Card: ❑ VISA, ❑ MasterCard, ❑ Optima, ❑ AMEX,
❑ Discover
Card number: ....
Name on card: .... Exp. Date: .... / ....

Call *toll free* and *order now*